"Blessed are those who revere the food they eat;
for reverence to food bestows strength and vitality."
Manusmriti

sukham ayu

Cooking at Home
with
Ayurvedic Insights

Jigyasa Giri & Pratibha Jain

wisdom
tree

Researched at KARE (Kerala Ayurvedic Research and Rejuvenation Establishment), Mulshi Lake, Pune, India

Fourth print May 2016

Disclaimer: This book based on Ayurvedic insights contains guidelines and suggestions for a healthy life through proper diet. It can neither replace your own inner intuition nor the benefits of direct consultation with a licensed Ayurvedic practitioner.

RESEARCHED AT KARE (Kerala Ayurvedic Research and Rejuvenation Establishment),
Mulshi Lake, village Gonawadi, Pune district, Maharashtra, India.
Email: info@karehealth.com
Website: www.karehealth.com

DESIGN TEAM
Direction Envission Communication & Kavitha Shivan

PHOTOGRAPHS Srivatsa Shandilya
PHOTO LOCATION KARE, Mulshi

© 2008 Jigyasa Giri & Pratibha Jain

ISBN 978-81-8328-312-0

Published by
Wisdom Tree
4779/23, Ansari Road
Darya Ganj, New Delhi-110 002
Ph.: 23247966/67/68
wisdomtreebooks@gmail.com

Printed in India

Like two
banks of a river, birth and death
are the boundaries of life. AYURVEDA, the
science of life, takes us beyond these banks. It is
anantapaaram - with no beginning and no end. Residing
forever in the lap of time, this great science of good health and
longevity is revealed from era to era to those who aspire to drink its
nectar of wisdom. It is believed that the complete science of Ayurveda
was born from Brahma, the Creator. It passed on to Lord Indra, the king
of the heavens - protector of all under his care. At the end of the *Satyayuga*
or 'Golden Era of Goodness', the noble sages who spent their lives in penance
and scriptural study gathered at the mighty peaks of the Himalayas to ponder
over the well being and longevity of human life. It was the time when disease
had crept into the human body and these sages worried about the sufferings
caused by ill-health. Thus it came to be that they sought the secrets of
Ayurveda from Lord Indra who revealed them for the benefit of all humanity.
It is from the words of many such seers that the Vedas - the four treatises of
knowledge, considered foremost and sacred - came into being in India.
These are the *Rig Veda, Yajur Veda, Sama Veda* and *Atharva Veda*.
Within the *Atharva Veda* are nestled the great texts of Ayurveda,
which are considered the primary sources of knowledge for
healthy life and happy longevity or SUKHAM AYU. Today
Ayurveda is acknowledged as a recognised science in
India. Its wisdom and insights have stood the
test of time, serving humanity at
every turn.

Benediction

Annam Param Brahma. Food being God, it is a great honour for me to express my feelings after reading the manuscript of "SUKHAM AYU - Cooking at Home with Ayurvedic Insights" (Researched at KARE) by Srimati Jigyasa Giri and Srimati Pratibha Jain.

Today, the entire world has become health conscious as well as diet conscious. As such, I find this is a very handy book as it deals with vegetarian recipes congenial to one and all.

We are aware of the adage "As you sow, so you reap". I'd like to add to this, "As you eat, so you are in your actions and thinking".

Though Sage Patanjali does not speak specifically on food, the way one has to prepare food and eat it, is hidden in the five moral principles of non-violence, truth, non-covetousness, chastity and non-greediness. The Mahanarayana Upanishad *and* Chandogya Upanishad *describe food as a pre-requisite to develop a healthy body, a sound mind and the power of speech. All the other Yoga texts dwell in detail on nourishing food as an essential requirement for progress in yoga, which has to be so chosen that it may not put unnecessary stress on the digestive organs.*

Just as yoga has to be learnt under the able guidance of a teacher, so also the preparation of food has to be learnt and prepared with a motherly touch of love, affection and compassion.

While Ayurveda or the science of life presents food according to one's constitution, yoga being a way of life, not only prescribes, but describes the ways of digestion and assimilation of food.

As the constitutional structure of each individual varies, my advice for all is to choose from this book what is good for you, keeping in mind that you must consume food while the salivary glands are stimulated, and stop eating the moment they go into respite.

This book contains details on sattvik food with appropriate presentation for each one to build up a healthy body with a sound mind. My best wishes and blessings to the authors for presenting a useful book on good food for all to choose from. My blessings to all the readers as they embark on this journey of good health and longevity.

Yogacharya B.K.S. Iyengar

An Invitation

The Ayurvedic approach to health is a participatory process, wherein the patient takes an active part in his own healing. He does this by conforming to a particular way of life according to his body constitution and other factors, the accent being on prevention rather than cure.

Although a doctor of modern medicine by qualification, I turned to Ayurveda in the year 1998 to heal my very own self of ailments caused by a way of life, quite unbalanced. My life was transformed within a short span of Ayurvedic treatment under the care of Dr. Nair. I became a new man radiating health and energy!

After my transformational experience, I converted my weekend farmhouse to a health retreat, now known as KARE. I was fortunate to find Mrs. Jaswandi Choudhary, who was trained in the Ayurvedic aspect of diet and nutrition at Pune University. With the guidance of our Ayurvedic doctors, chiefly Dr. Roli Rangappa, my aunt - Mrs. Usha Bail, my wife - Ragini, and indispensable feedback from our guests, we arrived at recipes and meal plans of simple, healthy and tasty food. It has been a long standing dream of mine to see these recipes featured in a cookbook that would help spread the message of Ayurveda.

As luck would have it, I met Jigyasa and Pratibha in Mumbai at Mr. Parigi's residence after the release of their book "Cooking At Home with Pedatha". I was very impressed with their book, and thus on an impulse, invited them to KARE in the hope of tempting them to bring out an Ayurvedic cookbook. That was an impulse I have never regretted.

Jigyasa and Pratibha have not only restructured the recipes from the KARE kitchen in a way that make them user friendly for daily home cooking, but have also added some along the way that we at KARE will be very happy to use. I thank them for their enthusiasm and commitment over the last two years, and for bringing my dream alive in the form of this wonderful book.

We are now in our tenth year at KARE and every year I am more and more grateful to the Almighty to have shown me this path of Holistic Healing. At KARE, nature plays a great role in the healing process along with traditional Ayurvedic therapies from Kerala, Iyengar medical yoga and Ayurvedic vegetarian cuisine according to individual body constitution.

I take this opportunity to invite the readers to visit KARE and experience first hand the magical healing therapies in the lap of Mother Nature, while enjoying sumptuous vegetarian Ayurvedic food.

Dr. Prakash Kalmadi
Founder and Medical Director, KARE

Our wanderings through the realms of our roots with our first book "Cooking at Home with Pedatha" prodded us to delve deeper into the treasures of traditional wisdom. It led us to the time when profound knowledge of health and well-being was sought and gathered by the Vedic sages through study and intuition. This body of extraordinary knowledge which they called Ayurveda, they passed on to their fellow human beings and their successors who, through generations, imbibed them as if they were inherent in their genes. So, our ancestors by instinct, and by the faith they placed in the knowledge of their **vaidya** *or physician, knew that the best medicine was always within reach - in the very food they ate.*

That was a different world.

Today, we seek Ayurveda mostly as information, as resource material. Looked upon more as a specialized branch of knowledge than as a way of life, it appears as though modern life has blurred it from our intuitive memories. Those masters who penned down their wisdom in the massive texts of Ayurveda have given us the chance not just to learn, but to inculcate within us the discipline of simple living and simple eating which is the key to good health and longevity. Through this cookbook, we hope that our readers will find a soft landing onto the path of a culinary balance in everyday life.

We were lucky indeed for, after Pedatha[1], we came into contact once more with a wonderful and enthusiastic human being, Dr. Prakash Kalmadi, a staunch believer in Ayurvedic principles. To spread the message of Ayurveda, he set up a beautiful and idyllic Ayurvedic rejuvenation establishment in the hill town of Mulshi in Maharashtra and named it 'KARE.'

KARE, pronounced as 'care', stands for Kerala Ayurvedic Research and Rejuvenation Establishment. Not far from the hustle and bustle of urban Pune, this Ayurvedic retreat is located in the Sahyadri range of the Western Ghats of India. The view of the tranquil Mulshi lake from the sunny cottages and moonlit terraces of KARE filled us with feelings of awe and oneness with nature.

This was the starting point for our project. Much as we have always liked reading the works of contemporary writers in the field such as Ms. Amadea Morningstar, Dr. Robert Svoboda, Dr. Scott Gerson and Dr. Vasant Lad, we never imagined that we would one day bring out a cookbook based on Ayurvedic insights. For that, above all else, our sincere gratitude goes to Dr. Kalmadi, his wife Ragini & their committed team, who introduced us to the Ayurvedic way of cooking, and the principles based on which the recipes at KARE have evolved.

---

[1] the protagonist of "Cooking at Home with Pedatha"

Apart from exploring the Ayurvedic tenets as expounded in texts such as 'Charaka Samhita' by Maharishi Charaka and 'Ashtanga Hridaya' by Maharishi Vagbhata, we also delved into 'Bhavaprakasha' by Acharya Bhava Mishra and 'Kshema Kutuhalam' by Acharya Kshema Sharma. These were our primary sources of reference. These treatises enveloped us into their pages as we began the process of learning from them. What can one say about the ocean of knowledge that lies there-in? We feel truly blessed to have sat by its shores, even if just to touch and be touched by its rippling waves.

About this book

*It has been our sincere endeavour to bring to you the great tenets of Ayurveda in simple, easy language and in a rhythm that we thought practical. As you turn these pages, you will find chapters that deal with different aspects of Ayurveda preceding each section of recipes. Thus, the first chapter "Who am I?" deals with the foremost dictum of Ayurveda, which places all of life within three categories of **doshas** or bodily humours - vata, pitta, kapha. This chapter is followed by a section on sweet dishes. The next chapter is "Self and the Elements" which deals with the connection between the five great elements and human existence, followed by a section on Soopa or soups. In this manner, sections of simple recipes are interwoven with compact pages of Ayurvedic teachings.*

More than anything else, this book aims to bring joy into cooking at home. It is, in a way, a culinary journey interspersed with ayurvedic insights, a peek into an ayurvedic system, each chapter leading you back home - with a basic home-style recipe. Although most of the recipes are for daily cooking, the home-style recipes are the first step into bringing Ayurveda and healthy, flavoursome cooking into your home.

*The recipe sections feature a selection of **tridoshik** preparations, which means that they can be eaten by persons of all constitutions (unless under supervised medical or diet treatment). However, any type of food is always more conducive to some and less to others, thus the popular proverb - one man's food is another man's poison. It is always interesting to know which foods one can eat regularly and which one should leave aside for occasional indulgences. So when you select a menu from this book for your family, all you have to do is identify who can eat more or less of each dish, based on the main ingredients.*

This is not as daunting as it may seem. When we sent a manuscript of these recipes to a friend to try out, she found that cooking and eating turned into a more conscious activity with the kids cheekily telling their kapha dad to go slow on the kheer, and the elder sister bossing over the younger one saying,"This salad is more for you than me!" What was really heart warming was when our friend said, "It somehow bound us all together and made eating time more fun!"

We hope that along with the tingling of your taste buds, this book kindles your curiosity to know more about this great science of life.

Jigyasa and Pratibha
December 2008

CONTENTS

>> All recipes in this book serve approximately four adults, quantity determined by the Ayurvedic principle of moderation.
>> General measures used in this book: teaspoon (5 ml), tablespoon (15 ml) and cup (200 ml).

WHO AM I? *prakriti*

We are born from a combination of the five elements that pervade the universe - earth, water, fire, air and ether. When sperm and ova unite, these elements are trapped into a biological form - each playing a vital role in the physiological and emotional formation of the life thus created. Earth, heavy and solid, constitutes our bone and muscle mass and keeps us emotionally and mentally grounded, while fire generates heat to allow metabolic processes like digestion to occur, and sets the stage for a fiery, aware and commanding mind. Water, the substance of all vital body fluids brings calmness and emotional succour. Air makes mobility within the body possible, gives us our life breath, lightens the spirit and allows for frivolous play of the mind. Ether, the subtlest of all, is the space in which our organs reside, giving us mental expanse and clarity.

This play of elements has been understood by the Vedic seers as the fundamental principle of Ayurveda. The elements predominate in pairs and give rise to the three doshas or tridosha which make up our 'prakriti' or constitution. A predominance of air and ether gives rise to vata dosha, that of fire and water to pitta dosha, and earth and water to kapha dosha. They are termed as dosha, which means flaws, simply because if not kept in balance, they are susceptible to vitiation thereby making the human body and mind vulnerable to disease.

Air + Ether	→	*Vata dosha*
Fire + Water	→	*Pitta dosha*
Earth + Water	→	*Kapha dosha*

The tridoshas are like three cups filled at different levels within the human body. The cup that is more filled than the others is that of your predominant dosha. The challenge is not to allow that cup to overflow, nor to allow the level in the other cups to drop too low, because ultimately they have to work together for the overall well being of the body and the mind.

Life is dear to all, and dearer still is a life of longevity, good health and well-being - thus the essence of Ayurvedic thought is based on **hitam ayu** *or a healthy life span, which is the pre-requisite for* **sukham ayu** *or happy longevity.*

Ayurveda teaches us to live a wholesome life that will keep the doshas balanced, the body healthy and the mind strong. It is a science that is based on understanding the individual and his constitution, his innate strengths and weaknesses; and how he can enhance the former and correct the latter through proper diet and life style. It is a medicinal science that treats illness no doubt, but more importantly, it teaches a way of life that enhances good health, longevity and vitality. Thus it is called the Science of Life; 'Ayu' meaning life, and 'Veda' meaning Science.

"Food when consumed without thought can be poisonous. The same when eaten with discrimination is the nectar of life."
Charaka Samhita

Pronunciation guideline:

Ayurveda - to be pronounced as 'aa-yur-veda'; with *u* as in *put*, *e* as in *they*, *da* as *the*

Kapha - *a* as in *spiral*, *ph* as in *pharmacy*

Pitta - as 'pit-ta', with *i* as in *pin*, *t* as in *path* (without stress on the 'h' sound)

Tridosha - with *t* as in *path* (without stress on the 'h' sound), *i* as in *pin*, *d* as *th* in *the*, *o* as in *pole*

Vata - as 'vaata', with *t* as in *path* (without stress on the 'h' sound)

Vata Dosha

The literal meaning of the word vata is 'that which moves'. In terms of our body constitution, vata displays the qualities of air and ether. Like air, it is dry, rough, mobile and light. And like ether, it is expansive, intangible and subtle. It is the originator of movements in the body, like respiration, circulation and excretion.

Vata dominant people tend to have a BONY and less muscular body frame, which can be maintained life long if not abused by improper lifestyle. Therefore vatas (i.e., vata types) do not, by nature, gain WEIGHT easily, but if they do, they can shed it off without much strain. They have dry skin and dark, visible veins. HAIR is always the bane of their life, being rough and often unmanageable. The dryness of the element air also causes NAILS and teeth of vatas to be rough. They tend to be very constipated and more often than not, are uneasy with a feeling of bloatedness.

Vatas display QUICK movements of eyes and limbs. They speak fast, eat fast and think fast. This comes from the quality of mobility of the element AIR. This mobility also manifests itself in the vata temperament. Vatas therefore have a rather frivolous nature, which isn't to say that they are 'scatter-brained'! But yes, they would probably tend to speak unnecessarily, jump in and out of MOODS, get angry at the drop of a hat and yet as quickly forgive and forget. Their RESTLESS nature makes them capable of changing BELIEFS easily, falling in and out of love, setting out to accomplish a task and then not completing it due to moving on to something new. They do not care to save for a rainy day and have an easy attitude towards earning and spending money.

They have light SLEEP, and often dream about jumping, falling, searching and travelling to unknown lands. They are very CREATIVE and their minds can travel on the wings of boundless IMAGINATION. But this very same capacity, when stretched, can also cause feelings of emptiness in heart and spirit and a sapping of mental and physical energy.

In conclusion…

Vata stress and trouble is kick started by worry, anxiety, cold and dry climates, erratic sleep and lack of routine. Vatas have low tolerance to physical pain, bright lights, loud noises and hunger pangs. Foods that have similar qualities to air and space aggravate vata. Dry, cold and astringent foods such as most legumes, cabbages, apples, raw onions, chillies and garlic in excess, do not agree with them. Such individuals are prone to air and ether related diseases. For example, the quality of lightness in air causes light sleep and can lead to insomnia in vatas. Likewise, constipation and joint pains arise from the quality of dryness of air; depression is also caused in them because of the 'void' that the ether is.

Vatas must find time for tranquility, stay warm, keep a routine, and eat warm and unctuous foods tempered with spices. In short, they should eat foods that are comforting but not unhealthy, and focus on achieving stability and purpose in life.

14

Pitta Dosha

The literal meaning of the word pitta is 'that which heats or cooks'. In terms of body constitution, pitta displays the qualities of fire and water. Like fire, it is hot, and sharp, with a strong odour, and like water it displays the quality of liquidity and viscosity. Pitta is responsible for all metabolic and chemical functions of the body like digestion, hunger, thirst, eyesight, body temperature and skin colour. It is also responsible for courage, jealousy and intellect.

Pitta dominant people tend to have a proportionate and attractive BODY FRAME. Warm to touch, they have a glowing COMPLEXION and a supple skin which can be maintained life long if not abused by improper lifestyle. Pittas have less body hair and a soft silky crown of hair on their head, often brownish or reddish in colour. On the flip side, strong BODY ODOUR is something they probably have to combat all the time and in some cases pitta males have low sperm counts. Pittas also have to deal with excessive SECRETIONS like urine, faeces and sweat.

Their penetrating EYES do not miss much and with the memory of an elephant, they retain all that they see and hear. Their sharp HUNGER pangs and quick-witted parlance reflect the fire element in them. They long for cool, airy CLIMATES, cool foods and drinks, and a lot of space to themselves.

Unlike the restless vata, they are firm and INTENSE in their feelings, beliefs and relationships. They give fully of themselves and expect the same of others. They are extremely GOAL ORIENTED, self motivated and ambitious, so God help the fool who would ever try to stop a pitta from reaching his or her goals! Not people who give in easily to temptations, pittas spend their hard earned money very carefully. With a forceful voice that can convey thoughts in a clear and assertive manner, they make good ORATORS and leaders because of their ability to influence others.

They have short but sound SLEEP and their dreams are intense, colourful, often relating to war, violence and anger. Intelligence, diligence, sharp memory and forceful speech are the big positives of pittas. If stretched beyond limits (which they invariably do to themselves), they find it very difficult to cope and can bite the head off the first person in their vicinity.

In conclusion…
Pitta stress and trouble is kick started by heat and humidity, heavy work load, frustration and anger. Pittas have low tolerance to stress, to the laid-back attitudes of others, closed, humid surroundings, and fiery foods. Sour, salty and pungent foods like yogurt, buttermilk, raw mangoes, tomatoes, raw onions, and chillies in excess irritate pitta. Such individuals are often prone to fire related diseases like fevers, ulcers and inflammations because of the fiery nature of pitta; heartburn, acidity, irritability and in extreme situations, heart attacks from stress, are some ailments that afflict these intense go-getters.

Pittas must find time to de-stress, retreat to cooler climes during hot summers and eat foods that are not too spicy or hot. Wheat, basmati rice, milk, non citric fruits and almost all beans are ideal for pittas. In short, they should eat foods that are calming and learn to master the art of moderation in all facets of life.

Kapha Dosha

The literal meaning of the word kapha is 'that which binds'. In terms of our body constitution, kapha displays the qualities of water and earth. It is responsible for lubrication and cohesion in the body. Like earth, it is solid, heavy, grounded and sluggish. Like water, it is soft, unctuous, sweet, cold and clear.

Kapha dominant people tend to have handsome or gentle features, a fair, almost pale COMPLEXION, and well lubricated skin, hair and joints which can be maintained life long if not abused by improper lifestyle. Their body structure is stocky and muscular giving them a heavy gait. They tend to gain WEIGHT easily and find it very difficult to shed it. There is a largeness about kaphas that comes from earth, and combined with the lucidity of water, it gives them their moist large EYES, thick eyelashes, silky hair and sparkling teeth and nails.

Kaphas have high potency and procreativity. Endowed with a calm countenance, they talk less and have a LAID BACK attitude to life. They prefer small meals at shorter intervals, which is a good thing, but the temptation to eat rich, gourmet FOODS is very hard to resist! Thus lethargy and obesity could be the bane of a kapha individual unless kept in check with regular exercise and diet.

Kaphas are even-tempered people, who do not fly off the handle like the moody vatas or fiery pittas. Instead, they are calm and STABLE in mind with a logical intelligence, dependable with a steadfast loyalty towards beliefs, and deeply attached in love, friendship and familial ties. With a pleasing, often melodious VOICE, these gentle ones could make good singers. Their laid back attitude makes decision taking a slow process, but once decided on a task, they see it to completion. Although they take time to grasp a situation or a lesson, once grasped, they RETAIN it forever.

Kaphas have long and prolonged SLEEP with dreams relating to romance and pathos. They like to own large houses, live in luxury and need the security of a hefty bank balance. Despite their love for comfort, they do not spend easily and like to accumulate WEALTH. They are masters at investing safely and sensibly.

In conclusion…
Kapha stress and trouble is kick started by lack of physical activity and lethargic lifestyle. Foods that are sour, salty, oily, cold and heavy such as fast foods, root vegetables, dairy products, iced beverages and sweets aggravate kapha dosha. Kaphas have a low tolerance to dampness and humid climates. Such individuals are prone to water related ailments like asthma, water retention, cough and cold, and earth related ailments such as lethargy, gluttony, tumours and arthritis.

Kaphas must find time for plenty of physical activity and variety in life. Eating hot and dry foods like millets, chillies and fenugreek will energize them and keep the balance. In short, they should eat stimulating foods and allow for change in their lifestyles to drive away their inherent lethargy.

SELF TEST *prakriti pariksha*

Having reached this point, it might interest you to arrive at an understanding of your prakriti. Of the three descriptions in the previous pages, the dosha that describes you best would be your predominant dosha. Based on the permutations and combinations of the three doshas, there can be seven types of prakriti or constitutions:

vata
pitta
kapha
vata-pitta (or pitta-vata)
vata-kapha (or kapha-vata)
pitta-kapha (or kapha-pitta)
sama prakriti

Purely single constitution, i.e., vata, pitta or kapha are seldom found; so also *sama prakriti* or 'balanced constitution' is very rare. Most of us are of dual constitution, for example, you may feel closest to the pitta description, and find that vata is not too far behind in describing many aspects of you. So, you are a pitta-vata, pitta being the predominant dosha followed by vata, the secondary dosha. Kapha would be the least filled cup, meaning the least troublesome one for you.

However, for all practical purposes, you will be referred to by your predominant dosha. So whenever Ayurvedic texts say something about pitta, it would apply to you whether you are a pitta-vata or pitta-kapha type.

On your right, is a simple self-test to determine your dosha. In every row, identify the attribute that describes you best in the years of your youth and early adulthood. Either note the number of points on a piece of paper or download this test from www.karehealth.com to tick on it directly. Think, reflect and try to be as accurate as possible. You may need to tick more than one point in some rows. When you have completed the test, count your points in each column. The one with the maximum number is your predominant dosha followed by the next.

Conduct the test more than once so that you are sure of all the answers. However, remember that this is only a basic self-test, solely dependent on the person taking the test, rather than an interactive one with the physician.

For a more definitive analysis, it is always advisable to consult a licensed Ayurvedic physician, who will be able to identify your dosha type by checking your *nadi* or pulse. The ticking of the pulse is a storehouse of information about your prakriti, which remains unchanged through the changes of your life. However, an unsuitable lifestyle can cause *vikriti* or vitiation of your dosha, which a good Ayurvedic physician can diagnose. Use the 'write to us' link on the above website to contact the doctors at KARE for any queries.

	VATA	**PITTA**	**KAPHA**
BODY FRAME	lean	well proportioned	broad and robust
BODY WEIGHT	cannot gain weight easily but can shed it rapidly	can gain as well as shed weight easily	can gain weight easily but cannot shed it as fast
SKIN TEXTURE	dry, rough to touch	soft, oily, warm to touch	thick, supple, cool to touch
COMPLEXION	dull, darkish skin	glowing skin, whether fair or dark	pale skin, whitish complexion
HAIR	dry and coarse	smooth and fine	silky and lustrous
FOREHEAD	small	medium	large
EYES	small and darting	medium and penetrating	large and attractive
APPETITE	enjoy munching between meals	intolerant of hunger, eat well during meals	like to eat small quantities of food at short intervals
THIRST	variable	excessive	scanty
STOOLS	frequently constipated, hard and gaseous stools	regular, soft and loose, often burning stools	regular, thick and oily stools
EXCRETIONS	Less sweating and urination	profuse sweating and urination, strong body odour	moderate sweating and urination
VOICE	weak, hoarse or shrill voice	commanding and sharp voice	gentle and pleasing voice
WORK	start impulsively, but do not necessarily complete tasks	highly task and goal oriented	slow to begin, but always see a task to completion
MIND	restless and easily distracted	passionate and generative	calm and stable
EMOTIONS	quick in emotional reactions and outbursts	intense emotions of like or dislike, love or hate	do not get angry, have calm endurance
TEMPERAMENT	forgive and forget easily	hold grudges for long	forgive, but never forget
RELATIONSHIPS	frequently in and out of love	enter into intense relationships	deeply attached in love and grounded in family ties
WEATHER	prefer sunny, warm and rainy climate	prefer cool, pleasant and airy climate	comfortable anywhere except in humid climate
MONEY	spend easily, do not care to earn or save much	plan well before spending	do not spend easily, like to accumulate
MEMORY	quick to learn and quick to forget	quick grasp and strong retention	slow grasp but strong retention
SLEEP	less and disturbed	less but sound	deep and prolonged
ROUTINE	dislike set routine	enjoy planning	set in routine
BELIEFS	radical or changing	intense, almost fanatic	loyal and steadfast
ACTIVITIES	like to be amidst action and movement	enjoy self-initiated activities	like serene and leisurely activities

We begin the recipes in this book with a sweet platter for your enjoyment. Food substances are identified by the six essences, which are sweet, sour, salty, pungent, bitter and astringent. As we enjoy these essences in the foods we consume, they affect us by their qualities, their potency, and their post-digestive effect (refer p.39).

Ayurveda teaches us that our digestive fire is at its peak around noon. So begin lunch with a sweet dish, the heaviness of which needs a strong digestive fire.

This section starts with **kshirika**, commonly referred to as 'kheer'. Milk and rice are the main ingredients of this nourishing preparation, which pacifies pitta and vata with its cooling, heavy properties. Rice can be substituted with other ingredients such as broken wheat, vermicelli, green gram, almonds or carrots. Try using **rock sugar** instead of refined, bleached sugar. Since sweets generally increase kapha due to their heaviness, it is a good idea to add spices such as cloves, cardamom and nutmeg to lighten them.

HOME-STYLE CARROT KHEER pic. on p. 27

Carrot 1 large, grated
Cow's milk 4 cups
Almonds 12-15
Cloves 2
Powdered rock sugar 4 tbsp
Cardamom powder ¼ tsp
Cow's ghee 1 tsp

1 Soak the almonds for 1 hour.

2 In a thick bottomed pan, bring the milk to a boil and allow to simmer.

3 Steam the grated carrot for 4-5 minutes. Set aside to cool.

4 Peel almonds and grind very coarsely. Now add the carrot and grind in one or two quick turns of the mixer.

5 In a wok, heat ghee and add the cloves. As they puff up, add the carrot-almond mixture and sauté for 1 minute.

6 Add to the simmering milk along with sugar and continue cooking over low flame for 7-8 minutes, stirring occasionally. Adjust sugar as per preference. Add the cardamom powder and switch off flame.

Serve in small quantity, either warm or at room temperature.

DATES KHEER

Pitted dates 15-20
Cow's milk 4 cups
Saffron 8-10 strands
Wheat flour 1 tsp
Nutmeg powder a pinch
Cardamom powder ¼ tsp
Cow's ghee 1 tsp

DATES have a sweet essence and post-digestive effect. They serve as thirst quenchers, body energizers, aphrodisiacs and also help increase levels of haemoglobin. Their sweet and moist qualities benefit vata and pitta. Add finely chopped dates to any kheer and reduce sugar accordingly. To balance the heaviness of dates for kapha, use nutmeg and cardamom as in this recipe.

1 Wash the dates thoroughly and chop fine.

2 Bring the milk to a boil and allow to simmer.

3 Prepare saffron by rubbing it in 1 tsp warm milk until the milk turns orange. Set aside.

4 In a thick bottomed pan, heat ghee, add dates and sauté for 2 minutes over low flame. Sprinkle wheat flour over the dates and sauté for another minute.

5 Now slowly add the milk, stirring continuously to avoid lumps and continue cooking over low flame for 7-8 minutes. Dates add their own sweetness to this kheer, but if you like it sweeter, add a dash of powdered rock sugar.

6 Stir the prepared saffron into the kheer along with the nutmeg and cardamom powders. Switch off flame.

Enjoy a small helping and stay light.

You can make any of the kheers in this collection using strained jaggery syrup instead of sugar. For kaphas, old jaggery is considered best among sweeteners. However, sometimes jaggery curdles hot milk. So cool the kheer before adding jaggery syrup.

If you like, add a very small pinch of powdered edible camphor along with sugar. It is cooling and adds its distinct flavour to kheers.

BROKEN WHEAT KHEER

Broken wheat ¼ cup
Cow's milk 3½ cups
Almonds and pistachios 6-7 each
Saffron (optional) 8-10 strands
Nutmeg powder a pinch
Cardamom powder ¼ tsp
Powdered rock sugar 4 tbsp
Cow's ghee 1 tsp

Many Indian sweets are prepared with milk. They can be made that much more wholesome if the milk comes from an animal that has been treated with tenderness and love, as the temperament of beings is reflected in their by-products. COW'S MILK which has a sweet essence and post-digestive effect is recommended by Ayurveda since it is easier to digest than milk obtained from other animals. Its heavy, stabilizing and strengthening qualities make it vata friendly while its cooling and unctuous properties calm pitta. Kapha adults need less milk and the best time for them to drink it is in the afternoons.

1   Soak the almonds and pistachios for 1 hour, peel and sliver.

2   Prepare saffron by rubbing it in 1 tsp warm milk until the milk turns orange. Set aside.

3   In a wok, heat ghee and sauté the broken wheat over low flame for 2-3 minutes. Transfer to a vessel that fits into a pressure cooker, add 1 cup water and cook for up to 3 whistles.

4   In a thick bottomed pan, bring the milk to a boil and allow to simmer for 4-5 minutes. Now add the cooked wheat and sugar and continue cooking over low flame for 4-5 minutes, stirring occasionally to avoid the grain sticking to the bottom. Adjust sugar as per preference.

5   Stir the prepared saffron into the kheer along with slivered nuts, nutmeg and cardamom powders and switch off flame.

Serve in small dessert bowls, either warm or at room temperature.

Make any of the kheers in this collection more flavoursome by adding ½ cup coconut milk at the end, just before switching off the flame. Reduce quantity of milk accordingly.

WHITE PUMPKIN HALWA

White pumpkin ½ kg
Cow's milk 2½ cups
Almonds 3-4
Cloves 3
Cashewnuts 3-4, chopped
Raisins 8-10
Rose water (edible) 1 tsp
Powdered rock sugar 4-5 tbsp
Cardamom powder ¼ tsp
Cow's ghee 1 tbsp

Ash gourd or WHITE PUMPKIN is sweet in essence, cooling and heavy. It is nourishing, has aphrodisiacal qualities and aids in healing blood related ailments. Tender pumpkins reduce pitta and vata. Mature pumpkins which are slightly alkaline in taste, stimulate digestive fire, cleanse the urinary bladder and mitigate all doshas. This recipe is enhanced in taste and nutritional benefit by a sprinkling of cool rose water.

1 Soak the almonds for 1 hour, peel and sliver.

2 Peel, grate and squeeze out most of the liquid from the pumpkin. The pumpkin should now measure approx. 1½ cups. The pumpkin liquid may be added to any soup or dal preparation if using immediately.

3 In a thick bottomed wok, heat ghee, reduce flame and add the cloves and cashews. Stir and when the cashews turn light golden, add the raisins. As they puff up, add the grated pumpkin. Sauté over medium flame for 5-7 minutes.

4 Now add milk and cook for 15-20 minutes, stirring constantly until the mixture thickens. Stir the rose water and sugar into the mixture and continue to cook until it becomes a soft fudge that rolls off the spoon easily.

5 Switch off flame and garnish with slivered almonds and cardamom.

Savour a warm helping, just enough to pacify the taste buds.

~ *Substitute pumpkin with bottle gourd, carrots (preferable the red variety) or coarsely ground fresh green peas.*

~ *For a richer halwa, reduce quantity of milk to 1 cup. Add ¾ cup khoya (unsweetened reduced milk) along with the sugar and proceed with the recipe.*

SWEET VERMICELLI

Vermicelli 1 cup
Almonds 3-4
Cloves 3
Cashewnuts 3-4, chopped
Raisins 8-10
Powdered rock sugar ¾ cup
Cardamom powder ¼ tsp
Cow's ghee 1½ tbsp

Dough of wheat flour is pressed through a fine sieve to make thin, noodle-like strips. These strips when dried are known as sevika or VERMICELLI. Nutritious like wheat, vermicelli provides the base for a wide range of Indian snacks and sweets. This recipe is a light and healthy sweet dish requiring less sugar and ghee when compared to most other Indian sweets.

1   Soak the almonds for 1 hour, peel and sliver.

2   In a thick bottomed wok, heat ghee. Reduce flame and add the cloves and cashews. Stir and when the cashews turn light golden, add the raisins. As they puff up, add the vermicelli. Sauté over medium flame for 7-8 minutes until the vermicelli turns deep golden.

3   Alongside in a pan, boil 2 cups water and the sugar. As the water starts bubbling, strain directly into the vermicelli. Stir continuously. Cook for 4-5 minutes until all the water evaporates. Switch off flame and garnish with slivered almonds and cardamom.

4   Cover with a tight lid and allow to stand for 5-7 minutes. Take off lid and gently fluff up the vermicelli.

Enjoy a small helping at the beginning of lunch and stay light.

KHOYA POLI *pic. on p. 37*

Wheat flour 2 cups
Cow's milk ½ cup
Cow's ghee 1-2 tbsp

The stuffing
Unsweetened khoya 1 cup
Bengal gram flour 1 tbsp
Nutmeg powder a pinch
Mace powder a pinch
Cardamom powder ¼ tsp
Powdered rock sugar ¾ cup

Reduced milk or KHOYA is used in the preparation of many Indian sweets. It is made by boiling milk over low flame and stirring almost continuously until it is reduced to a smooth, fudge-like consistency. Sweetened and unsweetened khoya (or mawa) is readily available in Indian stores and super markets. Like milk, it is nourishing, cooling and unctuous. Its heaviness is more easily handled by vatas and pittas. Flavouring it with spices, as in this recipe, allows kaphas to indulge in an occasional bite too.

1   For the stuffing, heat 1 tbsp ghee in a wok. Reduce flame and roast the bengal gram flour until its aroma rises. Add khoya and continue to sauté for 1-2 minutes. Stir the sugar into the khoya along with the spice powders. Sauté for 3-4 minutes and switch off flame when slightly thick and sticky. Cool and divide into 8-10 portions, roll into balls and set aside.

2   Make a soft dough with 1½ cups flour, milk and as much water (approx ¼ cup) as required in a broad, rimmed dish. Cover and set aside for at least 10 minutes. Place the remaining dry flour beside the dough.

3   Divide the dough into 8-10 portions and roll into balls. Flatten one ball and dip into the dry flour. Using a rolling board and pin, roll into a disc of 4 inch diameter. Place one ball of the stuffing on the disc and pack it in by pulling the edges together over it. Once sealed, dip into the dry flour and roll evenly into a poli of 4-5 inch diameter. Rolling lightly and evenly ensures the even spreading of the stuffing inside the poli.

4   Place the poli on a hot skillet over medium flame. Flip it over when small air bubbles appear on the surface. Flip 2-3 times, each time applying gentle pressure on the poli with a flat spatula or a piece of cloth held in your hand. When golden spots appear on both sides, lift the poli off the skillet. Repeat with the remaining dough.

Serve 1-2 polis per person, lightly smeared with warm ghee. Tangy Amti (p.61) makes a delectable accompaniment.

Once on the skillet, each poli takes approx. 3 minutes to cook. Make sure that the skillet does not become too hot and smoky as this will burn the polis. Ideally, the polis should be crisp rather than soft, but not hard.

To make the famous Puran poli, change the stuffing as follows: Pressure cook ½ cup bengal gram with ¾ cup water to a soft consistency. When cooked, churn into a soft, thick paste. In a wok, cook the gram paste and ½ cup strained jaggery syrup over low flame, stirring continuously. Flavour with spices like cardamom, nutmeg and mace. When it becomes thick and translucent in texture, and loses its stickiness, set aside to cool. Make the polis as in the recipe above.

SHRIKHAND

Fresh yogurt (from cow's milk) 4 cups
Almonds and pistachios 3-4 each
Rose water (edible) ½ tsp
Saffron 4-5 strands
Cardamom powder a pinch
Powdered rock sugar ½ cup
Charole nuts 2 tsp
Rose petals 7-8

1 Soak the almonds and pistachios for 1 hour, peel and sliver.

2 Tie the yogurt in a muslin cloth and hang over a bowl for 3-4 hours or until all the liquid from it has drained off, leaving it thick and creamy, measuring approx. 2 cups.

3 Transfer into a large bowl. Whisk the hung yogurt, rose water, saffron, cardamom and sugar into a smooth, creamy paste with a spatula. Adjust sugar as per preference. Garnish with the slivered nuts and charole and decorate with rose petals.

A delicious sweet dish, which can be eaten at the beginning of a meal or as an accompaniment to Roti (p.65).

We were excited when we came across praises for this delicious dessert in Ayurvedic texts, describing it as nourishing, unctuous and taste enhancing. SHRIKHAND increases potency, is sweet, cooling, energizing and acts as a laxative. It also alleviates thirst, burning sensations and common colds. It is good for vatas and pittas, but kaphas have to go slow on it just as they have to with all sweets. So enjoy this dessert but remember, moderation in everything is the magic word!

COCONUT BURFI

Fresh coconut 1 cup, grated
Beetroot ½ medium-sized, grated
Cow's milk 3 cups
Powdered rock sugar ¾ cup
Cloves 3-4
Nutmeg powder ¼ tsp
Cardamom powder ½ tsp
Cow's ghee 1½ tsp

The sweet and ripe COCONUT, an auspicious fruit in Indian ceremonies is heavy, strengthening and nutritious. Its cooling and unctuous properties reduce vata and pitta, but increase kapha. Used extensively in Indian food in its tender, ripe and dried forms, coconut is used in the preparation of the traditional 'coconut burfi', referred to in Ayurvedic texts as narikela khanda, a sweet dish said to be prepared by Dhanvantri, the God of Ayurveda himself. We end the sweet platter with this recipe made colourful and tridoshik with the addition of beetroot and spices.

1 In a thick bottomed wok, heat 1 tsp ghee and add the cloves. As they puff up, add the coconut, beetroot, milk and sugar.

2 Cook this mixture, stirring constantly over medium flame for 30-40 minutes. Cook patiently until the milk thickens and the mixture becomes a thick fudge that rolls off the spoon easily. Switch off flame.

3 Grease a metal tray with ghee. Transfer the coconut mixture to the greased tray and press it down evenly using the bottom of a flat bowl.

4 Sprinkle cardamom powder. When cooled, cut into bite-size squares.

Serve 1-2 squares at the beginning of a meal.

You may substitute beetroot with carrot in the above recipe.

Clockwise from top left:
Crushed ginger & salt (refer box, p.36)
Home-style carrot kheer p.19
Basic home-style vegetable with yam p.41
Green peas curry p.49
Basic home-style dal p.55
Basic home-style pulav p.75
Brahmi chutney p.96
Sprouts salad p.101
Centre: Basic home-style roti p.65
Outside thali: Home-style buttermilk p.102

SELF AND THE ELEMENTS *pancha mahabhuta*

"In the beginning was Space, from which came Air. From Air leapt Fire, and from Fire gushed Water. From Water emerged Earth, and from Earth's plants and seeds was born man."
Taittiriya Upanishad

Over centuries, seers have urged us to dwell on who we are, on what the "I" is that we identify with. Is it the body, is it the senses, is it the mind? You are all of these, the seers say, but you are also the Spirit, you are life eternal. Your spiritual energy is the spirit of the universe, your biological energy is the biology of the Universe. This is because everything flows from one Absolute Source. Thus, recognizing the universal law that human nature or prakriti is identical to the nature of the universe, Ayurveda offers the pathway to longevity and health by helping humans live in accordance with the laws of Nature.

Everything in the universe, including our bodies, is composed of the five Great Elements, known as the pancha mahabhuta. Our human form is the very Earth of the universe, and the fluids that flow within us are from the great element Water. Air, the vital force, is the breath of our being, and Ether is the space within us that allows the play of organs, fluids and emotions. Fire gives life and energy in the form of our body heat and digestive fire. And the unmanifest Brahman of the universe - He is the very spirit that dwells within.

EARTH *prithvi*

When we think of earth, we visualize lofty mountains, sprawling beaches and sand dunes in the deserts. This element gives us our nourishment since all plant life - our food - is rooted in the soil of mother earth. At a subtle level, it is this very same earth that gives the human body its solid form. It shapes our physical dimensions, constitutes our organs, bones and muscle mass and facilitates the sense of smell in us.

We experience the essences of sweet, sour and astringent when earth dominates along with water, fire and air respectively in the foods we eat. This is not all. It is that which keeps us grounded, not just physically, but emotionally and mentally too. Kapha qualities such as steadfastness and loyalty come to us from earth, the stoic element.

FIRE *tejas*

Fire is heat in any form. In nature, it is the lightning in the sky and the energy that burns forests. It is the heat of the sun that breathes life into plants allowing them to bear fruits. It is that which allows food to be cooked without and within our bodies. It generates metabolic processes like digestion and facilitates the sense of sight in us.

We experience the essences of sour, salty and pungent when fire dominates along with earth, water and air respectively in the foods we eat. It shapes the realms of our actions, spurring us to do rather than just be. It is that which sets the stage for a fiery, aware and commanding mind. Pitta qualities such as determination and will power come to us from fire, the element of intensity.

WATER *apa*

Water is the home for marine life in tranquil lakes and deep oceans. Water nourishes plants and keeps them turgid, transporting the earth's nutrients to all its leaves and fruits. Within our bodies, it is the substance of all vital fluids like blood, mucus and saliva, facilitating the sense of taste in us.

We experience the essences of sweetness and salinity when water dominates along with earth and fire respectively in the foods we eat. It also shapes our emotional being, nurturing the ebb and flow of feelings in our hearts. Kapha qualities such as cohesion and pitta qualities such as lucidity come to us from water, the graceful element.

AIR *vayu*

From the swaying of trees to the rotation of the earth, all movement in the universe is the blessing of this dynamic element, air. It holds within itself the life breath of the plant and animal kingdoms, facilitating the exchange of oxygen and carbon dioxide between the two. Air moves our limbs and joints and facilitates the sense of touch in us.

We experience the essences of pungent, bitter and astringent when air dominates along with fire, ether and earth respectively in the foods we eat. It transports blood through the veins, food through the digestive tract and thought waves through the mind. Air, the propelling element, shapes our mental make-up endowing us with vata qualities of creativity and flexibility.

ETHER *akash*

The elusive ether is the container of all that is. It is the urn in which the Creator created his magic - the planets, sun, moon, and galaxies unknown. Air, fire, water, earth and all their myriad forms find their place in ether. The carrier of sound and silence, this element is the void within our skeletal frame inside which reside and function our organs, pores, bones and tissues.

We experience the bitter essence when ether dominates along with air in the foods we eat. It is also the space within our minds that envelopes thoughts and observations. In the intangible space of the heart, it is the vessel of love and hate. As the co-element that makes up vata, it gives us mental expanse and clarity of thought, and above all, the quality of non-resistance through the channel of its infinite space.

As we see the omnipresence of the creator in the universe, so also do we see the universe within us. The presence of the cosmic elements in the human body is acknowledged in Ayurveda as its life force.

If you have sat by the ocean and felt the spray of the waves cleanse your being, or sensed your spirits rise with the blowing winds; if you have climbed mountains and felt yourself grow taller, or watched a bonfire and felt a surge of inspiration; if the expanse of the sky has filled you with space and distance from all stress and worry, then you have experienced the oneness that you share with the Elements and the Universe.

As Sage Atreya said to his student Agnivesha, "When we learn to appreciate the entire universe in the self and the self in the universe, we develop true intelligence. A mind filled with this knowledge shines as radiantly as the sun in a clear sky. It is the beginning of yogic endeavour. We learn to think, eat and live correctly."

It was quite interesting to note that Ayurvedic texts refer to a preparation known as **soopa**, which is very similar to the soups or broths that we are familiar with. There is a special reference to soopya shaak, or soups made from the leaves of pulses such as green gram and black gram. Thus we call the soups in this section by their Ayurvedic name - soopa. Ideal as a starter before dinner or as a warm winter-time drink, soopa is nourishing, refreshing and easy to digest.

Season all foods with powdered rock salt which is a preferred Ayurvedic choice over iodized table salt.

BASIC HOME-STYLE SOOPA pic. on p. 37

Bottle gourd 2 cups, peeled and chopped
Cloves 2
Garlic 2 cloves, chopped fine
Wheat flour 1 tsp
Cow's milk ½ cup
Pepper powder a generous pinch
Powdered rock salt to taste
Basil or coriander to garnish
Cow's ghee ½ tsp

1 Pressure-cook the chopped gourd in 1 cup water until soft. Churn in a blender, strain and set aside.

2 Make a smooth paste of wheat flour in ¼ cup water and set aside.

3 In a pan, heat ghee and add the cloves and garlic and sauté for 1 minute. Add the wheat flour paste, 1½ cups water, bottle gourd puree and milk. Bring to a boil and allow to simmer for 5 minutes. Season with salt and pepper.

Garnish with chopped basil leaves and serve 1 cup per person before dinner.

• Substitute bottle gourd with your choice of vegetables, like cabbage, chayote squash, corn, green peas, spinach, red pumpkin, white pumpkin, or any combination that helps balance your dosha (refer food guide p.108). If using cabbage, grind coarsely and do not strain the soup.

• You may substitute wheat flour with green gram flour or any millet flour like sorghum, maize, pearl millet or finger millet.

CARROT SOOPA

Carrots 2, chopped roughly
Onion 1 medium, quartered
Cloves 2
Garlic 2 cloves, chopped fine
Green chilli (optional) 1 small
Cow's milk ½ cup
Pepper powder a generous pinch
Powdered rock salt to taste
Coriander leaves 2 tbsp, chopped
Cow's ghee ½ tsp

1   Heat the ghee in a pressure pan. Add the cloves and as they puff up, add the garlic and onions and sauté for 2-3 minutes.

2   Now add carrots, chilli and 1 cup water. Pressure cook up to 1 whistle.

3   Cool, discard cloves and chilli and churn using a blender. Transfer into the same pressure pan, straining the soup if you so desire.

4   Add 1 cup water and allow to simmer over low flame for 7-8 minutes. Stir in the milk and coriander leaves, bring to a boil and switch off flame. Season with salt and pepper.

Garnish with coriander leaves and serve 1 cup per person before dinner.

CARROTS are sweet, bitter and astringent. Recommended for vatas and kaphas, they are nutritious and especially good for the eyes. Although their essences seem ideal, their sharp, heating qualities diminish their goodness for pittas, particularly in their raw state. Here is a healthy carrot soup well balanced with milk and coriander leaves.

VEGETABLE AND LENTIL SOOPA

Cabbage ¼ cup, shredded
Cauliflower 3-4 florets
Carrots 1 small, chopped medium
French beans 4-5, chopped medium
Onion 1 small, chopped fine
Garlic 2 cloves, chopped fine
Split green gram (husked) 2 tbsp
Pepper powder a generous pinch
Powdered rock salt to taste
Cow's ghee 1 tbsp

1 Pressure-cook the vegetables (except onions and garlic) along with green gram and 1 cup water for up to 1 whistle. Churn using a blender, strain and set aside.

2 In a pan, heat the ghee. Sauté onions and garlic over low flame for 2-3 minutes until onions start browning.

3 Pour the soup mixture into the onions along with 1 cup warm water and allow to simmer for 5-7 minutes.

Season with salt and pepper and start dinner with this hot soup.

Follow the recipe using bottle gourd, pumpkin, chayote squash or broccoli instead of a combination of vegetables.

The legend has it that Garuda, king of birds, when receiving divine nectar from Lord Indra, spilt a few drops of it on earth, from which grew the GARLIC plant. The ancient seers recommended this succulent, sharp and heavy bulb for its excellent medicinal properties even though it is not considered sattvik. It is rich in all essences except sour, since its seed is sweet, roots are pungent, leaves bitter, stem astringent and the apex of stem salty. It restores worn tissues and broken bones, keeps the heart healthy, strengthens vocal chords, stimulates digestive fire and is a terrific brain and eye tonic. Greatly beneficial to vatas and kaphas, pittas must have it in moderation and well cooked. Enhance the goodness of food with garlic as in this wholesome soup.

MILKY VEGETABLE SOOPA

Cabbage ½ cup, chopped fine
Carrot 1 small cup, chopped fine
French beans 4-5 cup, chopped fine
Shelled green peas 1 tbsp
Corn kernels 2 tbsp
Wheat flour 1 tsp
Cow's milk 2 cups, boiled
Pepper powder a generous pinch
Powdered rock salt to taste
Cow's ghee 1 tsp

1   In a pan, heat ghee and add the vegetables. Sauté for 2-3 minutes.

2   Slowly pour in 1½ cups milk and allow to simmer for 10-12 minutes until vegetables are cooked, but crunchy. Add ½ cup water if you find it too thick.

3   In the meanwhile, dry roast the wheat flour over low flame for 1 minute. Cool and mix it into the remaining ½ cup milk, making sure there are no lumps. Add this to the boiling soup.

4   Allow the soup to simmer for 2-3 minutes and switch off flame.

Season with salt and pepper and serve in small soup bowls. Since this soup has the richness of milk, you can follow it with a light dinner.

If counting calories, feel free to use skimmed milk instead of regular cow's milk.

*What makes a recipe tridoshik is the right combination of ingredients and the **samskara** or 'refinement' that they undergo in the cooking process. The vegetables in this soup have been chosen to balance the heaviness of milk which aggravates kapha. So if you are a kapha, enjoy this soup occasionally, and follow it up with a very light dinner. This soup is good for vatas and pittas, and a much recommended one for children.*

CLEAR SOOPA OF SPINACH

Spinach 1 heaped cup, chopped fine
Carrot 1 small, sliced
Garlic 2 cloves, chopped fine
Cumin seeds ½ tsp
Fresh lemon juice 1 tsp
Powdered rock salt to taste
Cow's ghee 1 tsp

1 In a thick bottomed pan, heat ghee. Add the cumin and as it begins to crackle, reduce flame and add garlic. Sauté for 1 minute

2 Add the carrots and sauté for 2 minutes. Toss in the spinach and stir for 1 minute.

3 Now add 3 cups water and salt. Allow to simmer for 7-8 minutes over low flame. Switch off flame and stir in the lemon juice. Serve hot, strained or otherwise.

Begin dinner with 1 cup of this healthy appetizer.

To make clear vegetable soopa, substitute spinach with mixed vegetables of your choice.

A grandmother moving a LEMON in a circle around her grandchild's face and chanting a mantra is not an uncommon sight in India. Lemon with its sharp qualities is believed to ward off the evil eye. The superstition probably came about because the lemon was understood as a fruit that has tremendous healing powers. For example, it is used in the elimination of worms, colic, indigestion, diarrhoea, dysentery and ailments that arise from imbalances of vata, pitta and kapha. Sour in essence and post-digestive effect, it is an appetizer as well as a digestive, beneficial to vatas and kaphas and moderately so to pittas. A dash of lemon juice added to food enhances taste and ignites digestive fire.

SPICY GINGER-LEMON SOOPA

Split red or green gram ¼ cup
Ginger 2 inch piece, crushed
Green chillies 2, slit
Turmeric powder a pinch
Coriander leaves 1 tsp, chopped fine
Fresh lemon juice 1 tbsp
Powdered rock salt to taste

The tempering
Cow's ghee 1 tsp
Mustard seeds ½ tsp
Cumin seeds ½ tsp
Asafoetida powder a pinch
Curry leaves 7-8

1   Pressure-cook the red gram to a soft consistency. Alternately, soak the gram in warm water for half an hour, strain and boil in 1 cup water in an open pan until soft. The gram need not be mashed or churned.

2   Add chillies, crushed ginger, turmeric powder, rock salt and 2 cups water and allow to simmer for 5-7 minutes. Strain and set aside.

3   In a wok, heat ghee for tempering and pop the mustard. Reduce flame and add the cumin, asafoetida and curry leaves. Pour this tempering into the simmering soup. Switch off flame and flavour with lemon juice and coriander leaves.

Try this warm and soothing drink during a cold winter evening. A healthy soup, it is much recommended during convalescence.

A sharp flavouring agent in many dishes, GINGER has a pungent essence and sweet post-digestive effect. Unctuous and hot in potency, it mitigates vata and kapha and is an effective purgative, relieving constipation, nausea and abdominal pain. Its sharpness and heating qualities can be handled by pittas only in moderation. Chewing on a teaspoonful of crushed ginger and salt before a meal, stimulates digestive fire and enhances taste. However, consuming fresh ginger is not advisable for those suffering from blood disorders, ulcers, acidity and fever. It is also better avoided during summer and autumn

Clockwise from bottom left:
Basic home-style soopa p.31
Khoya poli p.24
Stuffed paratha p.67
Broken wheat upma p.88
Rotla with millets p.69
Centre: Basic home-style chila p.85
Bottom centre: Home-style chutney p.95

THE ESSENCE IN FOOD *shad rasa*

What makes sweet foods agreeable to some and disagreeable to others? Why do some people suffer from acidity with chillies while others enjoy their spice without a problem? What are the right foods for each of us?

The ancient seers explained the connection between food and our doshas as the sheer magic of the five great elements. For, just as pairs of elements dominate in us to give rise to our doshas, so also they dominate in food substances to give rise to the *shad rasas* or six essences of sweet, sour, salty, bitter, pungent and astringent. The six essences are not just tastes of the palate, but have a dynamic connection to our doshas. They have twenty properties or *gunas* by which they affect our doshas, either mitigating or aggravating them. These properties make foods heavy or light, unctuous or dry, cooling or heating, dull or sharp, smooth or rough, dense or viscous, soft or hard, stable or mobile, gross or subtle, and clear or sticky.

If you look closely, you will find that these are the same properties that are found in our doshas also. For example, pitta is hot, light and sharp. Among essences, pungent essence is hot, light and sharp. Hence, by the formula of 'like increases like', pungent foods such as chillies, ginger and peppercorns aggravate pitta. Essences that have the opposite qualities will mitigate pitta, such as the sweet essence which is cold and heavy.

Typically foods with sweet essence increase kapha (some exceptions being old rice, old barley, wheat, green gram, honey and sugar), foods with sour essence increase pitta (except pomegranate and gooseberries), and foods with bitter and pungent essence increase vata (some exceptions being pointed gourd, dried ginger and garlic).

SWEET *madhura*

When earth and water dominate in a food substance, we taste sweetness. Sugar, rice, wheat, dates and milk are some foods which are sweet. Heavy, cool and unctuous, this essence evokes the emotion of desire in us. With the coolness of water, it quenches thirst and calms any fieriness within us, including irritated nerves and ruffled emotions. It has the heaviness of earth which strengthens our bodily tissues. This essence brings stability to the airy vata and coolness to the fiery pitta. Dominated by the same elements as kapha (earth and water), it has nothing much to offer to the kapha individual. Eaten in moderation and at the beginning of a meal, foods rich in sweet essence promise satisfaction and longevity in our lives. When consumed in excess, they cause discontent and yearning.

SOUR *amla*

When earth and fire dominate in a food substance, we taste sourness. Lemons, tamarind, kokam, citrus fruits and yogurt are some foods which are sour. This hot and unctuous essence helps balance the cool and dry vata. Its lightness gives us a sense of humour, allowing us to see life as a duality of sweet and sour. It stimulates digestive fire, adds zest to food and energizes the body. It also aids vata activity in the colon and helps in the elimination of waste products. Consumed in excess, sour foods provoke emotions of jealousy and envy. The unctuousness in sour essence makes it less beneficial for kapha. So also, pitta does not benefit from its heating property which can cause acidity and burning sensations in the throat and chest.

SALTY *lavana*

When fire and water dominate in a food substance, we taste the salty essence. It is considered the king of tastes because salt adds flavour to food, and in its absence, other essences cannot be enjoyed. Excessive consumption of chips and fast foods increases salt intake. The heaviness and moistness which this essence derives from water aggravates kapha, and the heat it derives from fire aggravates pitta. The light, dry and cool vata needs this essence the most. It aids digestion, clears the obstruction of channels and pores, and penetrates the tissues. It is said that life must be taken with just a pinch of salt. Consumed in excess, foods which are salty provoke within us the emotion of greed, aggravate thirst and heat, and can be the cause for premature wrinkling, greying and balding.

PUNGENT *katu*

When fire and air dominate in a food substance, we taste pungency. Chillies, peppercorns, garlic, ginger, onion, radish and mustard are some foods which are pungent. This sharp, hot and dry essence is much needed by kapha since it jolts the sluggish kapha complacency. Vatas must consume pungent foods in small quantities, just enough to stimulate digestive fire. Pungency has the power to stimulate digestive fire, and generate thought and action. Thus the fiery pitta does not need more of a sharp essence such as the pungent essence. It adds zing to food, promotes digestion and absorption, and helps in the elimination of sticky waste products. Consumed in excess, foods rich in pungent essence give rise to acidity, cause ulcers, and stimulate the emotions of aggression and anger.

BITTER *tikta*

When air and ether dominate in a food substance, we taste bitterness. Fenugreek, bitter gourd and turmeric are some foods which are bitter. Cool, dry and light, this essence is rich in medicinal value, serving as a hypoglycemic, germicidal and antitoxic agent. It mitigates pitta with its cooling properties and kapha with its light and dry qualities. On the other hand, it is the essence which is identical in qualities to vata dosha, and hence, is least needed by vatas. The bitter essence helps us face life's realities. In excess, it provokes pessimism and grief.

ASTRINGENT *kashaya*

When air and earth dominate in a food substance, we taste astringency. Gooseberries, pomegranate, red gram and raw bananas are some foods which are astringent. This essence is water absorbing, hence it causes thirst and dryness of mouth. Cool, heavy and dry, it purifies and tightens all pores of the body. Its coolness balances pitta and its dryness is good for kapha, but vatas need to minimize it in their diet. Consumed in moderation, foods which are astringent bring about a clear, uncluttered view of life. In excess, they evoke anxiety, fear, and emotional restriction. They also cause obstruction of urine, stools and semen, bringing about constipation, stiffness and weariness.

Food substances are endowed with a POTENCY, a capacity to have an effect on us when consumed. This is called *virya* which is of two kinds - hot and cold. Substances that have hot or high potency ignite digestive capacity and those with a cold or low potency subdue digestive capacity. Obviously then, food substances of hot potency, like most spices and yogurt, are less recommended for pitta which by itself, is hot, whereas they benefit vata and kapha. Substances that have a low or cold potency, like coconut and coriander, mitigate pitta while aggravating vata and kapha.

As soon as we eat, the first effect of food upon our bodies is through the essence itself. As food undergoes digestion, its potency affects our digestive capacity. And long after digestion, the effect continues with 'POST-DIGESTIVE EFFECT' or *vipaka*. In the stage of vipaka, the properties of foods sometimes undergo change and affect us accordingly. For example, honey is sweet in essence, but its vipaka which carries the properties of pungent essence is stronger. Thus this calms kapha despite its inherent essence of sweetness which is not otherwise kapha friendly.

There are some foods which may be similar in essence, potency and post-digestive effect, yet affect us differently. This inexplicable effect is known as *prabhava*. For example, ghee and milk are similar in *rasa-virya-vipaka*, yet ghee is a purgative while milk is not.

As we gain knowledge of foods, their essences, and their influences, we will learn to recognize which essences help balance which doshas, why a particular food substance suits one and not another, and why one man's food can truly be another man's poison.

Sprouts, yam, capsicum, bitter gourd, peas, drumsticks, cabbage - there is something in this section for everyone in terms of dosha compatibility and taste preference. Tempered with spices, these recipes are simple, healthy and tasty. Vegetables that are cooked without adding water to them tend to stick to the bottom of the wok while cooking. Therefore, cover the wok with a rimmed lid and pour some water over the lid during the cooking process. This prevents the vegetable from sticking to the bottom, yet allows it to cook in its own liquid. While lifting the lid, make sure that any water remaining on it does not fall into the wok.

Buy fresh vegetables, preferably those that are locally grown and in season. Greens are better avoided during the monsoon as they tend to be infested with grit and worms. Remember to wash all vegetables well before cooking them, paying special attention to herbs and leafy vegetables.

BASIC HOME-STYLE VEGETABLE pic. on p. 27

Any vegetable (see tip) 4 cups, chopped
Turmeric powder a pinch
Red chilli powder ½ tsp
Coriander powder 2 tsp
Powdered rock salt to taste

The tempering
Cow's ghee 1 tsp
Mustard seeds ½ tsp
Cumin seeds ½ tsp
Asafoetida powder a pinch

1   In a wok, heat the ghee for tempering. Pop the mustard and add the cumin. As the cumin starts crackling, reduce flame and add the asafoetida. Immediately, add the chopped vegetable and sauté for 2-3 minutes.

2   Add the turmeric, red chilli powder, coriander powder and salt. If using any of the vegetables from tip 1, reduce flame, cover with a rimmed lid and pour ¼ cup water on the lid. Within 3-4 minutes, check if the vegetable is cooked and switch off flame.

Garnish with coriander leaves and serve fresh with Rotla (p.69) and any Dal.

* Cook amaranth leaves, beetroot, bitter gourd, bottle gourd, cabbage, capsicum, carrots, fenugreek leaves, ivy gourds, onions, pointed gourd, pumpkin, ridge gourd, snake gourd, radish (with leaves), spinach or spring onions (with leaves) using this recipe. Among these, bitter gourds and ivy gourds may take a few minutes more to cook. General measure for greens in this recipe would be 5-6 cups when chopped.

* If using baby corn, cauliflower, cluster beans, corn, french beans, fresh green peas, raw plantains or yam, add ½ cup water after adding the spice powders. Cover and cook until the vegetable is done.

* You can also follow the same recipe using fruits like ripe guavas and apples! Add a dash of sugar along with the spice powders.

SPROUTS WITH YAM

Bean sprouts 1 cup
Fenugreek sprouts 2 tbsp
Yam 2 cups of ½ inch cubes
Turmeric powder a pinch
Red chilli powder ½ tsp
Coriander powder 1 tbsp
Cumin powder 1 tsp
Garam masala (refer tip p.49) ½ tsp
Coriander leaves ¼ cup, chopped
Powdered rock salt to taste
Cow's ghee 2 tsp

The paste
Onion 1 small, chopped
Garlic 1-2 cloves
Ginger 1 inch piece
Fresh coconut 1 tbsp, grated

1 Peel, wash and chop the yam into medium-sized chunks. Boil along with turmeric in a pan of water. When soft, strain and set aside.

2 Steam the sprouts for 5-7 minutes.

3 For the paste, heat ½ tsp ghee in a wok. Add the onions, garlic and ginger and sauté for 2-3 minutes. Grind into a fine paste along with coconut using very little water.

4 Heat the remaining ghee in the same wok. Add paste and sauté over low flame for 2-3 minutes. Add the sprouts, yam, chilli powder, coriander powder, cumin powder, garam masala, coriander leaves and salt along with ¼ cup warm water. Cover and continue to cook for 5-7 minutes until the water has evaporated. Switch off the flame.

Serve fresh with Rotla (p.69).

TO MAKE SPROUTS: Soak the required amount of green gram and fenugreek seeds overnight in a large bowl of water or for 6-7 hrs in warm water. Strain and place in sprout maker. Alternately, follow the traditional method of making sprouts by tying up the soaked lentil in muslin cloth. Hang this bundle on a hook with a bowl under it to collect any water dripping from it or simply place the bundle in a casserole once all water has drained off. Keep at room temperature or in a warm corner of your kitchen. After 10-12 hrs, the legumes will begin to sprout. Let them remain until the sprouts are ½ to 1 inch long. Ayurveda recommends that they should be blanched or steamed, and eaten in moderation.

SPROUTS are popular because they are rich in protein and make the lentil from which they sprout lighter to digest. Although readily available in super markets world over, they are easy to make and best eaten fresh rather than refrigerated. This recipe combines bean sprouts with the goodness of fenugreek sprouts and yam. In recent times, the fenugreek seed has become well known for its capacity to keep diabetes under control. It is heating, pungent-bitter in essence and helps to kindle digestive fire.

QUICK CAPSICUM

Green capsicum 4 medium-sized
Spring onions (with leaves) 1 bunch
Sorghum or green gram flour 2 tbsp
Coriander powder 2 tsp
Cumin powder 1 tsp
Red chilli powder 1 tsp
Coriander leaves to garnish
Powdered rock salt to taste

The tempering
Cow's ghee 1 tbsp
Mustard seeds ½ tsp
Turmeric powder a pinch
Asafoetida powder a pinch

1 Chop the capsicums into 1 inch squares and the spring onion bunch finely.

2 Dry roast the flour over low flame for 1-2 minutes until the aroma rises. Set aside.

3 For the tempering, heat ghee in a wok. Add the mustard and as it splutters, add the turmeric and asafoetida powders. Immediately, toss in the spring onions and capsicums, reduce flame and sauté for 2-3 minutes.

4 Sprinkle the roasted flour over the vegetable. Add coriander, cumin and chilli powders along with salt. Stir well, cover and cook for another 2-3 minutes.

Garnish with chopped coriander leaves and serve fresh with Roti (p.65) and any Dal from this collection.

You may substitute capsicum with fenugreek or spinach leaves.

Recommended for vatas and kaphas, the CAPSICUM is slightly pungent, thus increasing pitta. A new world favourite because of its crunchy, succulent texture, it is easy to use, easy to cook and enhances not just the flavours but also the look of salads, vegetables and pulavs. In this recipe, the cooling quality of sorghum or green gram flour and coriander leaves helps to create a tridoshik capsicum recipe.

TENDER DOUBLE BEANS

Fresh double beans ½ kg
Turmeric powder ½ tsp
Green chillies 2
Ginger ½ inch piece
Powdered rock sugar ½ tsp
Grated fresh coconut to garnish
Coriander leaves to garnish
Lemon juice 1 tsp
Powdered rock salt to taste

The tempering
Cow's ghee 1 tsp
Carom seeds 1 tsp
Asafoetida powder ¼ tsp

1   Shell the double beans. They should amount to approx. 2½ cups when shelled.

2   Add 2 cups water, turmeric and salt to the shelled double beans and pressure cook for up to 2 whistles or until the beans are soft but not overdone. Slightly mash a few of the beans by pressing them against the sides of the vessel to help thicken the gravy.

3   Pound or grind the chillies and ginger together coarsely.

4   In a wok, heat ghee for tempering. Add the carom and as it crackles, reduce flame and add the asafoetida.

5   Immediately add chilli-ginger paste, sugar and the cooked beans. Allow to simmer over low flame for 10-12 minutes until the gravy thickens slightly.

6   Stir in the coconut and coriander leaves. Add freshly squeezed lemon juice and switch off flame.

Serve fresh with Rotla (p.69) or Home-style Pulav (p.75).

Double beans look like flat beans, only broader, with thick outer jackets. While the jacket of the flat bean is tender and edible, double beans have to be shelled in much the same manner as green peas. All BEANS of the 'dolichos lablab' family are classified as having a sweet essence and post-digestive effect. Cooling, heavy and strengthening, they mitigate vata and pitta. With the warmth of spices like carom and ginger, they can be enjoyed by kaphas in moderation.

You may substitute double beans with ridge gourd. Omit steps 1 and 2, and proceed with the recipe. Add salt and turmeric along with chilli-ginger paste in step 5.

STUFFED POINTED GOURD

Tender pointed gourd ¼ kg
Cow's ghee 1 tbsp

The stuffing
Fresh coconut ½ cup, grated
Coriander leaves ½ cup, chopped
Goda masala (p.92) 1 tsp (optional)
Dry mango powder (amchur) ¼ tsp
Turmeric powder a pinch
Red chilli powder ¼ tsp
Coriander powder 2 tsp
Cumin powder 1 tsp
Asafoetida powder a pinch
Powdered rock salt to taste

1 Wash and pat dry the pointed gourds. Nick the ends and make a vertical slit in the centre to stuff. Scoop out hard seeds, if any.

2 Mix together all the ingredients of the stuffing. The moistness from the coconut and freshly washed coriander leaves is enough to bind the mixture. Now pack this stuffing into the gourds.

3 Heat ghee in a non-stick wok and gently place the gourds into it. Reduce flame, cover with a rimmed lid and pour ¼ cup water on the lid. This prevents the gourds from sticking to the bottom. Cook for 7-8 minutes, checking and stirring occasionally. While lifting the lid, make sure the water does not fall into the wok. If the water evaporates before the vegetable is cooked, add more water on the lid. Switch off flame when well done.

Serve fresh with Roti (p.65) and any Dal from this selection.

You may substitute the gourd with tender lady's finger, lemon-sized onions (making criss-cross cuts on top for stuffing), small capsicums (by carving out the stalk and scooping off the seeds) or tender bitter gourds (halved and slit like the pointed gourds, adding jaggery in the stuffing if you like).

POINTED GOURD is sometimes referred to as the king of vegetables. This is probably due to the fact that it has a good blend of rasas and qualities that render it healthy and tridoshik for consumption. Hot and light in quality, its firm and succulent texture makes it perfect for a savoury or a sweet stuffing. Its bitter essence and pungent post-digestive effect are balanced well in this recipe with a dash of tangy dry mango powder, a popular Indian seasoning.

TOSSED VEGETABLES IN MILK

Carrot 1 large, sliced diagonally
Cauliflower 10-12 florets
French beans 10, sliced diagonally
Shelled green peas ½ cup
Cow's milk ½ cup
Peppercorns ½ tsp, crushed
Mustard paste (or powder) ¼ tsp
Powdered rock salt to taste
Cow's ghee 1 tsp

1 Blanch the chopped cauliflower, strain and set aside.

2 In a wok, heat the ghee. Add all the vegetables and sauté for 2-3 minutes. Reduce flame and add milk.

3 Cover with a lid and allow to simmer for 5-7 minutes, stirring occasionally, till the milk thickens and coats the vegetables. Add the mustard paste and mix well.

4 Season with salt and pepper and switch off flame.

Garnish with coriander leaves and serve as an accompaniment in a meal.

Here is a simple and nourishing preparation, sans all the usual masalas of Indian cooking. Sweet carrots, milk and pepper balance the flatulence caused by beans, peas and cauliflower in this recipe. PEPPER which is dry, hot and sharp mitigates vata and kapha. It cures abdominal pain, and stimulates digestion. MUSTARD is also hot and sharp and adds zest to the creamy flavour of milk in this tridoshik combination of vegetables.

TANGY BITTER GOURD

Bitter gourds ¼ kg
Onion 1, chopped fine
Dry mango powder (amchur) ½ tsp
Turmeric powder ¼ tsp
Coriander powder 2 tsp
Cumin powder 1 tsp
Red chilli powder ½ tsp
Bengal gram flour 1 tbsp
Jaggery (optional) 2 tsp, grated
Roasted groundnuts 2 tsp, crushed
Coriander leaves to garnish
Powdered rock salt to taste

The tempering
Cow's ghee 2 tsp
Cumin seeds ½ tsp
Asafoetida powder a pinch

1 Chop the bitter gourd into thick round disks and remove hard seeds.

2 In a non-stick wok, heat the ghee for tempering. Add the cumin seed and as it begins to crackle, add asafoetida powder. Immediately, reduce flame, add the onions and gourds and sauté for 2-3 minutes.

3 Cover and cook for 5-7 minutes, stirring occasionally. Sprinkle a little water once or twice. Now add the remaining ingredients (except groundnuts and coriander leaves) and cook for 2-3 minutes.

4 Switch off flame and garnish with groundnuts and coriander leaves.

Serve fresh as an accompaniment in a meal.

Substitute bitter gourd with lady's finger or raw plantains. Omit the jaggery and groundnuts. For raw plantains, you may need to add a little more ghee.

Mature raw mangoes are peeled, chopped and dried under strong sunlight until completely dry. The powdered form of mangoes dried thus is called AMCHUR. Sour, sweet and astringent in essence, amchur works as a mild laxative. Readily available in Indian stores, it stays good for months if preserved in a cool, dry place and adds a delectable tang to many a dish. Bitter gourds which are good for pittas and kaphas, absorb the flavour of amchur and other spices in this recipe, making it possible for vatas to enjoy this dish too.

GRAVIED DRUMSTICK

Drumsticks 2, large
Thick tamarind pulp 2 tsp
Turmeric powder ¼ tsp
Red chilli powder ½ tsp
Powdered rock salt to taste
Coriander leaves to garnish

The tempering
Cow's ghee 1 tsp
Cumin seeds ½ tsp
Garlic 4 cloves, crushed
Asafoetida powder a pinch

1   Chop drumsticks into 3-4 inch long pieces, peeling off thin layers of the hard, fibrous skin as you chop.

2   In a wok, heat the ghee for tempering. Add the cumin and as it begins to crackle, add the crushed garlic and asafoetida.

3   Immediately reduce flame and add the drumsticks, tamarind pulp, chilli powder, turmeric powder, salt and 1½ cups of water. Cover and cook for 5-7 minutes. Take off the lid and continue to cook until some of the water evaporates, leaving a sauce like gravy.

Serve fresh, garnished with coriander leaves. An excellent accompaniment to Roti (p.65) and any dal.

As its name suggests, the DRUMSTICK is slender and long with a beautifully striated thick, almost corky outer skin. Sweet and astringent in essence, it enhances appetite, clears worms, relieves colic and is used in the cure of skin diseases. Most suitable to pitta and kapha, and moderately so to vata, it is described as 'deepanam param' which means that it stimulates digestive fire to its highest.

Drumstick cannot be cooked without its thick skin. However, it is only the inner pulp and seeds that are to be eaten and the skin chewed upon and discarded. During one of our meals at KARE, a guest who had never eaten drumsticks was flummoxed for she could not figure out how to eat it without feeling like a cow! Some of us took turns to demonstrate the act of scraping it in an outwardly direction between our teeth, chewing on the piece of drumstick while still holding it in our fingers and finally discarding it, having consumed the pulp and seeds. Eventually she did master the art and this rather funny-sweet incident made us realize how culture-specific food etiquette can be.

GREEN PEAS CURRY

Shelled green peas 2 cups, boiled
Turmeric powder ¼ tsp
Coriander powder 2 tsp
Cumin powder 1 tsp
Red chilli powder 1 tsp
Garam masala (refer tip) ½ tsp
Mint leaves 1 tbsp, chopped fine
Coriander leaves to garnish
Powdered rock salt to taste
Cow's ghee 1 tbsp

The paste
Onion 1 medium, chopped
Garlic 3-4 cloves
Ginger 1 inch piece
Fresh coconut 2 tbsp, grated
Pumpkin or sunflower seeds 1 tbsp

1 For the paste, heat ½ tsp ghee in a wok. Add the onions, garlic, ginger and the seeds and sauté for 2-3 minutes. Grind into a fine paste along with coconut using very little water.

2 In another wok, heat the remaining ghee. Add the paste. Reduce flame and sauté for 2-3 minutes.

3 Add the turmeric, coriander, cumin and chilli powders, and continue to sauté for 2-3 minutes until the ghee separates from the paste.

4 Add the boiled peas, mint leaves, salt and 1 cup warm water. Cover and allow to simmer for 4-5 minutes. Switch off flame and garnish with garam masala and fresh coriander leaves.

Serve fresh as an accompaniment to Mint Rice (p.76) or Masala Poori (p.70).

TO MAKE GARAM MASALA: Dry roast ¼ cup coriander seeds, 1 tsp cumin seeds, 1 tsp black cumin seeds, 3 bay leaves, 3 cinnamon sticks, 6 cloves, 3 black cardamom and 6 peppercorns over low flame until their aromas rise. Cool and grind into a fine powder and store in an air tight container.

Green PEAS are cooling and have a sweet-astringent essence. Intake of these little green pearls is beneficial to the pitta and kapha constitution. Since they have a tendency to cause dryness and flatulence, they are best eaten well spiced and in moderation by vatas.

AMARANTH AND GREEN GRAM

Amaranth leaves 1 large bunch
Split green gram (husked) ¼ cup
Onion 1, chopped fine
Turmeric powder ¼ tsp
Coriander powder 1 tbsp
Powdered rock salt to taste

The tempering
Cow's ghee 1 tsp
Cumin seeds 1 tsp
Garlic 3-4 cloves, crushed
Dry red chillies 2-3
Asafoetida powder ¼ tsp

1 Soak green gram in warm water for half an hour.

2 Discard thick stems from greens and wash well. Make sure that you remove all the grit from the leaves. Chop roughly and set aside.

3 In a wok, heat ghee for tempering. Add the cumin and as it begins to crackle, add the garlic, chillies and asafoetida. Reduce flame, add the chopped onion and sauté for 3-4 minutes.

4 Add the soaked gram (along with water), turmeric, coriander powder, ½ cup water and salt. Stir, cover with lid and allow to cook for 7-8 minutes until the gram is cooked, yet remains whole.

5 Now add the chopped greens and cook for 3 minutes. Switch off flame.

Serve fresh with Roti (p.65) in a meal.

You may substitute amaranth with spinach, fenugreek leaves or sunberry greens in the above recipe.

AMARANTH leaves are of many varieties, some green, others red, some with a sweet essence and post-digestive effect, and others with a bitter-sweet essence and pungent post-digestive effect. They are cold, light and dry and thus increase vata and to some extent kapha as well. Pitta on the other hand is mitigated by most leafy greens. In this recipe, the addition of the tridoshik green gram makes it a well balanced preparation for all.

CABBAGE KOFTA

The koftas

Cabbage 2 cups, shredded fine
Coriander leaves ¼ cup, chopped
Ginger-garlic paste 1 tsp
Green gram flour ½ cup
Red chilli powder ½ tsp

The paste

Onions 2 small, chopped
Watermelon seeds (optional) 2 tsp
Dry red chillies 2
Coriander seeds 1 tbsp
Poppy seeds 1 tbsp
Fresh coconut 2 tbsp, grated

Others

Cumin seeds ½ tsp
Asafoetida powder ¼ tsp
Turmeric powder a pinch
Garam masala (refer tip, p. 49) a pinch
Dry mango powder (amchur) ¼ tsp
Powdered rock salt to taste
Cow's ghee 1 tbsp

1 Mix all ingredients of the kofta along with salt and knead into a soft dough, without adding any water. Divide this dough into 4-5 portions. Grease your palms with a little ghee and roll each portion between your palms into 2 inch thick cylindrical rolls.

2 Place these rolls in a vessel that will fit into a pressure cooker. Steam (without the weight) for 8-10 minutes. Cool and chop into ½ inch thick pieces.

3 Heat 1 tsp ghee in a non stick pan, place koftas on pan and roast over medium flame for 10 minutes, flipping them over once or twice until lightly browned. Set aside.

4 Heat 1 tsp ghee in a wok and sauté the ingredients of the paste (except coconut) for 3-4 minutes. Cool and grind into a fine paste along with coconut using very little water.

5 In a large wok, heat the remaining ghee. Add the cumin and as it begins to crackle, add asafoetida powder and the ground paste. Reduce flame and sauté for 3-4 minutes. Add the remaining spice powders, 2 cups water and bring the gravy to a boil. Allow to simmer for 3-4 minutes.

Add koftas to the gravy and serve immediately with Rotla (p.69).

KOFTAS are generally fried dumplings. They are a popular and much loved addition to festive meals. You can get as creative as you like by making koftas out of almost anything from greens to grams. In this recipe, the steamed dumplings of cabbage are no less tasty than the traditionally fried ones. The vata increasing cabbage is calmed by the coriander, gram and spices. Quick and easy to make, it is a must-try recipe. You can also substitute cabbage with bottle gourd, or a combination of vegetables like carrots, french beans, cauliflower and spinach. Grate the cauliflowers and chop the others finely. Steam the vegetables and drain out all liquid before making the koftas.

FOOD AND THE SEASONS *ritucharya*

Nature is a genius juggler as she synchronizes our lives, our doshas, the great Elements, the seasons, planetary influences and all substances into a harmonious orchestra of co-existence.

According to Ayurveda, there are six seasons in a year, and each one makes its grand entry into our world exerting its influence on the doshas. As the seasons and essences intertwine with each other, doshas undergo accumulation, aggravation and mitigation within us, and in the atmosphere. The conjunction of the last seven days of the outgoing season and first seven days of the incoming one is known as 'ritu sandhi'. It is best to start giving up the foods of the outgoing season and acclimatize oneself to foods of the incoming season.

With global warming and ecological mayhem, it is difficult to demarcate the exact dates of seasonal change in modern times. But as long as the birds and beasts know by instinct the onset of new seasons, this golden advice of seasonal adaptation in our lives must prevail. The ancient seers declared that a person whose life-style is guided by seasonal regimen or 'ritucharya' benefits in strength, nourishment and radiance.

Late Winter, Spring and Summer are said to be sun dominant seasons, or in the phase of uttarayana. In this phase, all substances and living organisms undergo progressive depletion of energy and moisture. Monsoons, Autumn and Early Winter, are the seasons that fall under the phase of dakshinayana. This phase, beginning with the monsoons, revitalizes the body after the harsh summer months of energy depletion.

LATE WINTER *shishir*

The latter half of winter is the coldest season of the year, colder and drier than the first half of winter. Just as it is darkest before dawn, so also this season marks the end of the cool months and the beginning of the warm seasons. Kapha is slowly accumulated in the atmosphere and in substances during these months. Therefore, it is beneficial to start shifting to kapha balancing foods in this season, particularly if it is your predominant or secondary dosha. Avoid cold drinks and cold foods. The cold and dry weather allows for a moderate amount of sweets and fats in your diet.

SPRING *vasant*

Spring is a time of pollen and greenery, a season of romance. The accumulated kapha of late winter is now aggravated and dulls the digestive fire within us. Thus, it is time to be cautious of kapha related ailments. For example, asthma is aggravated in the season of spring when there is pollen in the air. Avoid sleeping at day time, as it increases lethargy in the already heavy kapha. Likewise avoid heavy, unctuous, sweet, cool and sour foods. Instead enjoy sharp, dry, pungent, astringent and bitter foods such as bitter gourd, fenugreek, ginger, wheat and green gram.

SUMMER *grishma*

Summer is the time when energy depletion is at its height as the heat of the sun overpowers everything in its wake. It dries up moisture in the atmosphere, in all water bodies and substances. The heavy and unctuous kapha is now mitigated and calmed. Vata begins to be accumulated in this season, yet it is time to be cautious of pitta related ailments such as heat stroke, fatigue, dehydration, ulcers and rashes. Avoid salty, sour, pungent and hot foods. Instead cool the body with sandal paste and enjoy juicy fruits, rice preparations, buttermilk, coriander leaves, honey, rose water, and fluids flavoured with camphor which mitigate pitta. Avoid excessive physical exercise, and direct exposure to the harsh rays of the sun.

MONSOON *varsha*

When the peacocks dance and the cuckoos sing, it is time for the rains to wash the earth. Monsoon is a time of low digestive fire and weakness, the body having been depleted of strength and energy in the phase of uttarayana. One often experiences burning sensation after digestion of food due to predominance of sour essence in the atmosphere and in all food substances. In the rainy season, vapour that is formed when the rains touch the summery earth, increases all doshas. Therefore, more diseases afflict beings now than in other seasons, so eat all foods in moderation. But remember that it is vata that needs to be balanced the most. Eat foods such as rice, barley, wheat, yogurt, lentil soups, and juices sweetened with honey. It is also advisable not to stay in the sun or sleep under dewy skies. Take it easy, avoiding strenuous exercise and work.

AUTUMN *sharad*

Autumn follows the monsoons and the restored vitality in the human body is further strengthened, as unctuousness increases in plants and humans. Pitta, accumulated in monsoons, now comes in contact with the sharp autumn sun, and is aggravated yet again. So just as in summer, eat sweet, bitter and astringent foods. Foods that calm pitta such as ghee, jaggery, barley, wheat, rice, green gram, pointed gourd, bitter gourd and gooseberries, and sweets made with milk and flavoured with camphor are recommended in this season. Enjoy the cool rays of moonlight in the early hours of the night, but do not sleep outdoors.

EARLY WINTER *hemant*

Early winter is the time of good health and rejuvenation as it is the final phase of the period of liberation. This is a period of cold, and snow in some regions of the world. It is the time when sweetness and unctuousness increase in plants and humans, bestowing strength and well being. Eat foods like wheat, rice, black gram, sesame, saffron, milk, and sugarcane products. This is the season when your body can digest fats like ghee and edible oils better. Enjoy the rays of the sun and warm yourself with bonfires after sunset. Dress warmly, massage the body with sesame oil and eat hot and spicy foods in this season. Pitta is calm, and it is vata that needs to be attended to. After this period, remember, another new year and another cycle of seasons begins once more with kapha accumulation.

Doshas undergo mitigation or aggravation all the time - not just during the various stages of digestion and during changing seasons of the earth, but also in passing hours of the day, and through milestones of an individual's life from infancy to old age.

Symbolized in the human form, kapha with its traits of chubbiness and need for comfort, is like a cherubic child. It is most predominant during infancy and early childhood, and on a daily basis, soon after meal intake, in the wee hours of the morning and early hours of night. Spring is the season of kapha predominance.

Fiery pitta, symbolized in the human form is an aggressive go-getter. It predominates in the middle years of life when one grows from youth into adulthood and middle age. On a daily basis, it is also most predominant 1-2 hours after meal intake, at midday and midnight. Summer is the season of pitta aggravation.

Vata is the shift from hard working middle age to the gentle slowing down of old age. On a daily basis, it is most predominant 3-4 hours after meal intake, at the end of the day and during the last phase of night. Winter is the time of vata predominance.

Although the doshas are present throughout our being, their seats of predominance in our bodies are also placed systematically wherein, kapha is predominant in the region above the umbilicus, pitta, is seated at the umbilicus and vata resides below the umbilicus.

One wonders at the precision of the Maker as He created these pillars of human existence in the form of childlike springy kapha, energetic summery pitta and frail wintery vata.

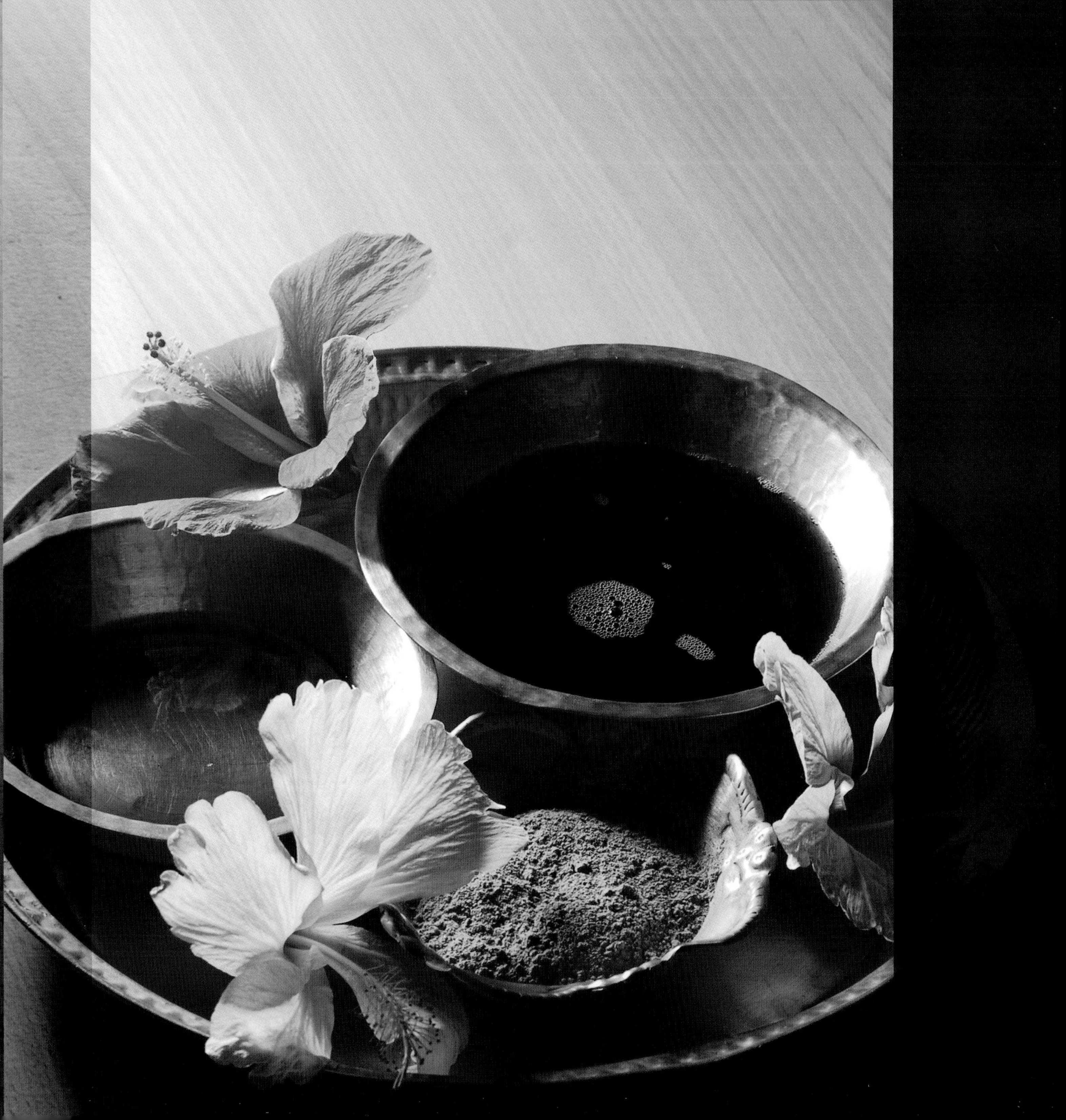

This section features 'dals' made from pulses or lentils like red gram, green gram, masoor or bengal gram. Rarely is an Indian meal complete without a dal which makes a delicious accompaniment to rotis and rice.

There are many options to choose from when one wants to add a sour tang to a dal such as tamarind pulp, lemon juice, tomatoes, raw mangoes, dry mango powder (amchur), yogurt or kokam. Among these, tomatoes are not recommended because of the high level of neuro-toxins contained in them. Of the remaining, there are clear cultural and regional preferences that determine the choice. It would be a good idea to use that which grows regionally since such a choice is most beneficial to health (refer p.62).

BASIC HOME-STYLE DAL *pic. on p. 27*

Split green gram or red gram ½ cup
Turmeric powder ½ tsp
Fenugreek seeds 8-10
Coriander leaves to garnish
Powdered rock salt to taste

The tempering
Cow's ghee 1½ tsp
Cumin seeds 1 tsp
Asafoetida powder a pinch
Curry leaves 5-6
Green chillies 2, slit

1 Pressure-cook the gram along with turmeric and fenugreek in 1½ cups water to a soft consistency. Churn well and set aside.

2 In a wok, heat ghee for tempering. Add the cumin and as it crackles, add the asafoetida, curry leaves and chillies.

3 Reduce flame, add the cooked gram and salt. If you find the dal too thick for your liking, add ¼ cup water. Allow to simmer for 5-6 minutes. Garnish with coriander leaves and switch off the flame.

Serve fresh. This dal is ideal for the entire family as part of a wholesome meal.

• *Spike up this simple dal by adding 1 finely chopped onion and a dash of ginger-garlic paste into the tempering. Sauté for 2-3 minutes before adding the gram. If using red gram, add 3-4 washed and soaked kokams along with gram for a tangy flavour. If using green gram, add a dash of lemon just before switching off flame.*

KOKAM KADHI

Dry soft kokam 6-8 pieces
Wheat flour 1 tbsp
Red gram 1 tbsp, powdered
Green chillies 2-3, slit
Jaggery 1 tbsp, grated
Coriander leaves to garnish
Powdered rock salt to taste

The tempering
Cow's ghee 1 tsp
Mustard seeds ½ tsp
Cumin seeds 1 tsp
Asafoetida powder ¼ tsp
Red chilli powder ½ tsp

1   Wash and soak the kokam in ½ cup warm water for half an hour.

2   In a pan, make a smooth paste of the wheat flour and powdered red gram with ½ cup water. Add kokam (with the water it was soaked in), green chillies, jaggery and salt along with 3 cups water. Churn lightly and bring to a boil, stirring till it thickens. Reduce flame and allow to simmer for 8-10 minutes.

3   In a wok, heat ghee for tempering. Pop mustard and add the cumin. As the cumin crackles, add the asafoetida and chilli powder.

4   Immediately pour this tempering into the simmering kokam kadhi. Switch off flame and strain the kadhi just before serving.

Garnish with coriander leaves and serve fresh with any rice preparation from this collection.

The raw KOKAM fruit is used extensively in many parts of India to add sourness to a recipe. While the unripe sour fruit is used in cooking, ripe kokam which is sweet-sour in essence is preserved as a concentrate, the diluted juice of which is recommended as a cooling summer drink. Kokam is light, dry and heating, and displays a sour post-digestive effect. Vatas are well benefited by this fruit, but pittas and kaphas would be better off with moderate consumption, the essence of sourness rarely being their best companion. Adding flour of finger millet to this kokam preparation makes it friendly and healthy for all.

You may substitute wheat flour with flour of bengal gram, green gram, finger millet, pearl millet or sorghum.

BOTTLE GOURD DAL

Bottle gourd ¼ kg

Bengal gram ½ cup

Dry soft kokam or tamarind pulp 4-5 pieces or 2 tbsp

Jaggery (optional) ½ tsp, grated

Coriander powder 1 tsp

Red chilli powder ½ tsp

Coriander leaves to garnish

Powdered rock salt to taste

The tempering

Cow's ghee 2 tsp

Mustard seeds ½ tsp

Cumin seeds ½ tsp

Curry leaves 3-4

Turmeric powder ¼ tsp

1   Wash and soak the gram in 1½ cups water for 15-20 minutes. Pressure cook along with the water for 2 whistles.

2   Wash the kokam and soak for 10 minutes. Peel and chop the gourd into medium-sized cubes just before tempering to avoid discolouration. This should amount to approx. 1 cup.

3   In a thick bottomed pan, heat ghee for tempering. Pop the mustard and add the cumin. As the cumin crackles, add the curry leaves and turmeric. Reduce flame and add the chopped gourd and ½ cup water. Cover and cook for 4-5 minutes.

4   Now add kokam, jaggery, coriander powder, chilli powder, salt and cooked gram. Continue to cook for another 7-8 minutes. Switch off flame.

Garnish with coriander leaves and serve fresh with Rotla (p.69) and steamed rice in a meal.

The juice of BOTTLE GOURD is highly recommended for daily intake. Sweet in essence, nourishing and good for the heart and tissues, it mitigates all the doshas. Select a gourd which is neither too tender for that will increase vata and kapha, nor one that is too ripe as that will increase pitta.

GUJARATI DAL

Split red gram ½ cup
Turmeric powder ½ tsp
Dry soft kokam or tamarind pulp 4-5 pieces or 2 tbsp
Jaggery 1-3 tsp, as per preference
Hard dry dates (optional) 4, halved
Drumstick 4-5 pieces, 2 inch length
Yam 4-5 pieces, 1 inch cubes
Groundnuts 1 tbsp
Green chillies 2, slit
Ginger 1 inch piece, chopped fine
Coriander powder 2 tsp
Cumin powder 1 tsp
Garam masala (refer tip, p. 49) ¼ tsp
Coriander leaves to garnish
Powdered rock salt to taste

The tempering
Cow's ghee 2 tsp
Mustard seeds ½ tsp
Fenugreek seeds ¼ tsp
Cumin seeds ½ tsp
Dry red chillies 2
Asafoetida powder ¼ tsp
Curry leaves 5-6

1   Wash and soak red gram for half an hour. Pressure-cook in 2 cups water along with turmeric to a soft consistency. Churn well.

2   Pour the churned gram into a thick bottomed pan and add all the ingredients (except garam masala, coriander leaves and tempering). Add 1 cup water and allow to simmer over low flame for 15-20 minutes, stirring occasionally.

3   In a wok, heat ghee for tempering. Pop the mustard and then add the fenugreek. Reduce flame and with the browning of the fenugreek, add cumin, red chillies, asafoetida powder and curry leaves.

4   Pour this tempering into the simmering dal. Allow to boil for another 5 minutes. Switch off flame and garnish with garam masala and fresh coriander leaves.

Serve fresh as a tasty accompaniment to steamed rice and Roti (p.65) in a meal.

RED GRAM is a popular lentil in Indian cooking. It is sweet-astringent in essence and pungent in post-digestive effect. Although heavy, it is best suited to kapha because of its dryness and astringency. Moderately suited to pitta, it is less favourable to vata because it causes flatulence and needs to be balanced with spices as in this recipe.

DAL WITH MIXED LENTILS

Split masoor gram ¼ cup
Bengal gram 2 tbsp
Split green gram (husked) 2 tbsp
Split black gram (husked) 1 tbsp
Turmeric powder ¼ tsp
Onion 1 large, chopped fine
Dry mango powder (amchur) ½ tsp
Coriander leaves 1 tbsp, chopped
Powdered rock salt to taste
Cow's ghee 2 tsp

The paste
Coriander seeds 2 tsp
Cumin seeds 1 tsp
Dry red chillies 3
Cinnamon 2 sticks, 2 inches long
Black peppercorns 3
Cloves 2
Garlic 2 cloves
Ginger 1 inch piece
Coriander leaves 1 tbsp, chopped

1   Mix the grams, wash and soak for ½ an hour. Pressure-cook in 3 cups water along with turmeric to a soft consistency. Churn lightly and set aside.

2   Grind the ingredients of the paste using as little water as needed.

3   Heat ghee in a thick bottomed pan. Add onions, reduce flame and sauté until they turn light pink.

4   Add the paste and continue to sauté for 3-4 minutes. Add dry mango powder, cooked gram, 1 cup warm water and salt and allow to simmer for 5-7 minutes.

Garnish with chopped coriander leaves and serve fresh with Home-style Pulav (p.75).

Most legumes such as aduki beans, broad beans, chick peas, black-eyed beans, dried peas, flat beans or kidney beans can substitute the mixed lentils in this recipe. These need to be soaked overnight.

MASOOR (red lentil) and GREEN GRAM are considered superior among lentils. Both cook well and are flavoursome. Sweet-astringent in essence, they balance pitta and kapha. Of the two, green gram is more conducive to vata. However, vatas need to balance the cool, dry qualities of most lentils by consuming them well cooked in spices. In this recipe, the medley of lentils and spices makes it a wholesome and welcome inclusion in a lunch menu.

BITTER GOURD DAL

Bitter gourd 1 large
Split red gram ½ cup
Turmeric powder ¼ tsp
Thick tamarind pulp 1 tbsp
Jaggery 1-3 tsp, as per preference
Goda masala (p.92) 1 tsp (optional)
Cumin powder ½ tsp
Red chilli powder ½ tsp
Dry coconut 1 tbsp, grated
Coriander leaves to garnish
Powdered rock salt to taste

The tempering
Cow's ghee 1-2 tsp
Mustard seeds ½ tsp
Asafoetida powder a pinch

1 Pressure-cook the red gram along with turmeric in 1½ cups water.

2 Chop the bitter gourd into thick round disks and remove hard seeds. In a pan, boil along with 1½ water until just cooked.

3 Now add the cooked gram, tamarind, and the remaining ingredients (except coriander leaves and tempering), reduce flame and continue to cook for 7-8 minutes, stirring occasionally.

4 In a small wok, heat ghee for tempering. Add the mustard and as it begins to splutter, add the asafoetida powder. Pour this tempering into the simmering dal. Switch off flame after 2-3 minutes.

Garnish with coriander leaves and serve fresh as an accompaniment in a meal.

Instead of dry coconut, you may add fresh coconut just before switching off the flame.

"May the fruit of BITTER GOURD reside in every morsel of mine." This sutra from Kshema Kutuhalam extols the qualities of bitter gourds which are known for their medicinal properties. They help in easing symptoms caused by ailments such as diabetes, anaemia, worms and even fevers. Bitter and pungent in essence with a pungent post-digestive effect, this vegetable is cold and light to digest and is most suitable to pittas and kaphas. It is an effective purgative, kindles digestive fire and is good for the heart. Along with the spices and dry coconut in this recipe, it can be enjoyed by vatas in small quantities.

TANGY AMTI

Split red gram ½ cup
Turmeric powder a pinch
Thick tamarind pulp 2 tbsp
Jaggery 1 tbsp, grated
Goda masala (p.92) 2 tsp
Red chilli powder ½ tsp
Grated fresh coconut to garnish
Coriander leaves to garnish
Powdered rock salt to taste

The tempering
Cow's ghee 2 tsp
Mustard seeds 1 tsp
Fenugreek seeds ¼ tsp
Asafoetida powder ¼ tsp
Curry leaves 4-5

Ripened TAMARIND, an essential flavouring fruit in south Indian cooking, has a sour essence and post-digestive effect. It is dry and heating, heavy to digest and does not aggravate any of the doshas. However, tender or raw tamarinds can aggravate pitta and kapha, so go slow on them if you have a predominance of either of these doshas. Here is a milder version of the traditionally spicy and tangy Amti, a popular preparation from Maharashtra.

1   Wash and soak the red gram for half an hour. Pressure-cook in 1½ cups water along with turmeric to a soft consistency. Churn well and set aside.

2   In a thick bottomed pan, heat ghee for tempering. Pop the mustard and add the fenugreek. Reduce flame and with the browning of the fenugreek, add the asafoetida and curry leaves.

3   Immediately, add the remaining ingredients (except coconut and coriander leaves) and 1 cup warm water. Allow to simmer for 5-6 minutes.

4   Switch off flame and garnish with coconut and chopped coriander leaves.

Serve fresh with Khoya Poli (p.24) or steamed rice.

Add a few pieces of drumstick or onion chunks into the tempering for added flavour. Allow to cook before continuing with step 3.

When in season, you can substitute tamarind with sour raw mango. Add 6-7 slices into the tempering and allow to cook before continuing with step 3.

FOOD COMPATIBILITY *satmya*

Is it that a pure and simple relationship exists between man and the food he eats? Or do we have to keep in mind many aspects of food in order to reap its benefits? The answer is in the latter wherein the theory of 'satmya' or compatibility with substances resides.

Just as a strong and beautiful relationship grows when there is compatibility between individuals, so also good health is gained when we eat foods that are compatible with us. This is satmya, the underlying principle of Ayurvedic dietetics. It weaves itself around several factors, such as region, climate, quantity, rasas, seasons, state of health and habits.

Compatibility by Habit *okasatmya*

When we eat certain foods as a regular habit for years or generations, the body adjusts to that food, making it compatible for itself. For example, tamarind is used in almost every dish in south India to bring sourness to food, although in other regions kokam or lemons are preferred. This is because, tamarind grows naturally in south India and the people who hail from this region have, over centuries, adapted to it. Sometimes, even incompatible or 'opposite foods' become compatible to us due to habitual intake. Although this does not justify their consumption, the fact remains that they are better digested by those who are used to them than by those who are not.

Geographical Compatibility *desh satmya*

Eat locally grown natural foods because foods which belong to a particular region are well suited to the long standing inhabitants of that place. When you go on a long holiday or relocate to another place, allow your body to adjust gradually to the foods of that region. As your system internalizes the new weather, culture and surroundings, geographical compatibility will set in, allowing those local foods to become agreeable to you over time.

Likewise, food substances are more beneficial if consumed in similar climatic conditions of their origin. Although modern technology has made it possible for food substances of cold climates to be exported to the warm plains, yet their benefits are more visible on those who inhabit the cold places.

Seasonal Compatibility *ritusatmya*

The best foods are those that grow naturally in any particular season. For example, watermelons in summer and water chestnuts in winter. Off-seasonal foods, preserved in cold storage, have little or no value in terms of their benefits on our bodies. In these days when chemically induced crops are available all round the year and all round the globe, seasonal compatibility seems like a remote idea. But our bodies have sensed the un-naturalness of the non-seasonal foods, and thus we see a renewed interest in organic farming, or of going back to natural foods.

Quantitative Compatibility *raashi*

Only an appropriate quantity of food ignites the digestive fire and increases longevity without aggravating the doshas. This is quantitative compatibility - neither too little nor too much. The secret to good health lies in the middle path, away from the extremes of starvation and indulgence. And yet, we may ask, how is one to decide the perfect quantity? Each person is unique, with his or her own height, weight, age and corresponding nutritional requirements. So is there a common answer? The sages who had the simplest of answers to baffling questions, said, "Let your palms be the measure. Let that much enter your stomach as much as can be held in your palms." No wonder then, that the bhikshus accept alms, even to this day, in their palms.

INCOMPATIBILITY *asatmya*

Just as some people cannot get along with each other try as they may, so also, some foods simply do not mix well, although they may be independently beneficial to us. According to Ayurveda, there are certain foods which, when combined, become incompatible and therefore detrimental to good health. One may not experience the negative or positive effects of food instantly or tangibly, but if one carefully observes how the body responds to food, then one will learn that the effects of certain food combinations are best avoided.

The reasons for incompatibility are many and varied. In some instances, the heating potency of one substance does not respond well to the cooling potency of another; for example, horse gram and milk. Likewise, some substances are considered harmful when mixed in equal quantities, such as honey and ghee.

Some combinations to be avoided:

Combining milk with citrus or sour fruits, such as plums, gooseberries and tamarind is not advisable. Sour or raw jackfruits, mangoes, bananas, pomegranate, and coconut are not compatible with milk. (Pitted dates and sweet, ripe mangoes can be safely combined with milk).

Avoid drinking milk soon after consumption of radish, drumstick, garlic or holy basil.

Combining milk and legumes such as moth beans, horse gram, black gram and broad beans is not advisable.

Yogurt should be avoided at night, but if consumed, it is best to mix it with sugar, dal made of green gram, honey or gooseberries. It should not be cooked because its properties become detrimental to us when heated. Ayurvedic texts say that buttermilk can be heated, but not yogurt. There is a mention of kvathita which is a soup made by heating a mixture of flour, buttermilk and spices. This is the popular 'kadhi' of north India.

Honey and ghee should never be mixed in equal proportions.

Honey and hot water should not be mixed together. Heating of honey is considered very harmful. Ayurvedic texts state that honey can even be heated by the body, when consumed by a person suffering from a heat stroke, thus making it unhealthy!

Apart from these combinations, it is important to eat right foods at the right time. Foods that increase vata do not provide adequate nourishment to a toiling labourer. Similarly, foods that increase kapha will only increase lethargy and obesity in one who leads a sedentary life. Consuming cold and dry substances in cold weather, or hot and pungent substances in warm weather are considered incompatible.

Thus, one must eat in accordance with one's prakriti or constitution, life style, seasons, age, geographical location, habits and personal health conditions. And above all, remember that for food to be compatible, it is not enough that it be fresh and tasty. It must also please all the senses. It should smell good, look good and feel good. As Charaka says, to eat that which is not pleasing to the senses is 'hridaya viruddha', which means incompatible with the heart.

A dough of wheat flour and water when rolled into a thin crepe and cooked over burning coal is known as **rotika** in Ayurvedic texts. This is the Phulka or Roti that we cook over a gas stove in the new world! The gas stove may remove some of its goodness, but generally Rotis are strengthening, nourishing and wholesome. They are recommended for all doshas; however, wheat being heavy, kaphas are advised to consume rotis made of wheat in smaller quantities.

To make a perfect roti takes some amount of practice, but once mastered, these grainy breads, lightly smeared with warm ghee, are delicious. The secret lies in getting the dough right. With practice, you will find that the softer your dough is, the softer your Rotis will be.

Typically, Rotis and Parathas are served directly from the skillet to the plate by the lady of the house as her family begins its meal. But if you make them in advance, wrap them in cloth and place in a casserole to keep them warm and soft.

BASIC HOME-STYLE ROTI *pic. on p. 27*

Whole wheat flour 2 cups
Cow's ghee ¼ tsp

1 Make a soft dough with 1½ cups wheat flour and as much water as required (approx ¾ cup) in a broad, rimmed dish. Rub a little ghee on your palms towards the end of the kneading process to smoothen the dough. Cover and set aside for 10-15 minutes. Place the remaining flour beside the dough.

2 Divide the dough into 10-12 equal portions and roll into balls. Flatten one ball and dip into the dry flour. Using a rolling board and pin, roll into a round roti of 6-7 inch diameter using light and even pressure. You will need to dip it in the dry flour once or twice to make the rolling easier. Each time, dust off all excess flour from it.

3 Transfer the roti onto a hot skillet over medium flame. Within seconds, when small bubbles appear on the surface, flip the roti on the skillet using a tong. Increase flame to high.

4 In a few seconds larger air bubbles will appear. Lift the roti off the skillet and flip it directly over the flame. As soon as it puffs up, take it off the flame. For vatas and pittas, you may brush a little ghee on it. Repeat with the remaining dough. Serve hot with any vegetable and dal from this selection.

- *FLAVOURED ROTI: Add 2 tbsp chopped mint and coriander leaves, a sprinkling of carom seeds, ¼ cup milk and salt while kneading the dough. Reduce quantity of water accordingly. These rotis can be made thicker than the traditional roti.*

- *CRUNCHY KHAKRA: Add ½ tsp carom seeds, 1 tbsp sesame seeds and a little salt while kneading the dough. Roll into thin rotis. After turning the roti twice on the skillet, reduce flame and keep pressing down on it, starting with the edges and moving into the centre in a circular movement with a flat wooden press. Flip over, repeat on the other side until light brown and crisp. Store in an airtight container and savour as a wholesome snack.*

FENUGREEK PARATHA

Wheat flour 2 cups
Bengal gram flour 1 tbsp
Fenugreek leaves ½ cup, chopped
Coriander leaves ¼ cup, chopped
Yogurt from cow's milk 2 tbsp
Turmeric powder ¼ tsp
Coriander powder 2 tsp
Cumin powder 1 tsp
Red chilli powder 1 tsp
Asafoetida powder a pinch
Powdered rock salt to taste
Cow's ghee 2-3 tbsp

WHEAT, the staple food of north India has a sweet essence and post-digestive effect. It is a nourishing vitalizer, bestows good complexion and increases potency. It is sadasevaniya, which means it can be included in everyday diet. According to Charaka, although wheat is sweet, it is an exception to the rule and does not aggravate kapha when eaten in moderation.

1   In a broad, rimmed dish, mix 1½ cups wheat flour and all other ingredients using only 1 tsp of the ghee. Knead into a firm dough using very little water. Cover and set aside for at least 10-15 minutes. Place the remaining flour beside the dough.

2   Divide the dough into 10-12 portions and roll into balls. Flatten one ball between your palms. Dip into the dry flour. Using a rolling board and pin, roll into a disc of 6-7 inch diameter. You will need to dip both sides of the paratha lightly into the dry flour once or twice to make the rolling easier.

3   Transfer the paratha onto a hot skillet over medium flame. When small air bubbles appear, flip, smear ¼ tsp ghee on the surface, making sure not to leave any dry spots. Flip again and press gently with a flat spatula, moving it on the skillet so that it does not stick. Now smear ghee and flip once more. When dark golden spots appear on both sides take it off the skillet. Repeat with the remaining dough.

Serve hot or wrap in cloth and place in a casserole.

Substitute fenugreek leaves with spinach or mint. Finely grated vegetables such as cabbage, bottle gourd, carrot or beetroot also make good substitutes. If using bottle gourd, remember to squeeze out some of its liquid before kneading the dough.

Add a sprinkling of nigella, sesame, fennel or poppy seeds for an occasional change in flavour.

STUFFED PARATHA *pic. on p. 37*

Wheat flour 2 cups
Powdered rock salt a pinch
Cow's milk ½ cup
Cow's ghee 1-2 tbsp

The stuffing
Split green gram (husked) ¾ cup
Mustard seeds ¼ tsp
Asafoetida powder a pinch
Turmeric powder a pinch
Coriander powder 1 tsp
Cumin powder 1 tsp
Red chilli powder ¼ tsp
Ginger (optional) 1 tsp, grated
Coriander leaves 2 tbsp
Powdered rock salt to taste

Ayurvedic texts refer to PARATHAS stuffed with cooked and spiced bengal gram or black gram as vetika. These stuffed parathas are a tasty and wholesome preparation, much relished during cold winters in northern India. Green gram, the best among lentils, is our choice of stuffing in this tridoshik recipe.

1 Wash and soak the gram for ½ an hour in 1 cup water.

2 For the stuffing, heat 1 tsp ghee in a wok and pop the mustard. Add asafoetida, turmeric and then the soaked gram (along with the water). Add just enough water to cover the gram. Cook over medium flame for 10-12 minutes, stirring occasionally until almost all the water evaporates and the gram is cooked, without becoming a mash. Add the coriander powder, cumin powder, chilli powder, ginger, coriander leaves and salt. Stir over low flame for 2-3 minutes. This stuffing should be soft, but dry.

3 Make a soft dough with 1½ cups flour, milk and as much water as required (approx ¼ cup) in a broad, rimmed dish. Cover and set aside for at least 10 minutes. Place the remaining dry flour beside the dough.

4 Divide the dough into 8-10 portions and roll into balls. Flatten one ball and dip into the dry flour. Using a rolling board and pin, roll into a disc of 4 inch diameter. Place approx 1 tbsp stuffing on the disc and pack it in by pulling the edges together over it. Once sealed, dip into the dry flour and roll evenly into a paratha of 4-5 inch diameter.

5 Transfer the paratha onto a hot skillet over medium flame. Flip it over when small air bubbles appear on the surface. Smear up to ¼ tsp ghee on the surface, making sure not to leave any dry spots. Flip again and press gently with a flat spatula, moving the paratha on the skillet so that it does not stick. Now smear ghee and flip once more. When dark golden spots appear on both sides, take it off the skillet. Repeat with the remaining dough.

Serve 1-2 parathas at lunch with any yogurt-based salad (p.100-101).

CAULIFLOWER STUFFING: *Substitute the soaked gram with finely grated cauliflower. Since the cauliflower is grated and cooks in its own liquid, there is no need to add water while making the stuffing.*

YAM STUFFING: *A nutritious and tasty substitute to the popular potato parathas. Substitute the soaked gram with ¼ kg cooked and mashed yam. Since the yam is already cooked, there is no need to add any more water while making the stuffing.*

RED PUMPKIN POORI

Red pumpkin ¼ kg or ¾ cup, grated
Wheat flour 1½ cups
Jaggery 1/3 cup, grated
Nutmeg powder ¼ tsp
Cardamom powder ¼ tsp
Powdered rock salt ¼ tsp
Cow's ghee for deep frying

We were pleasantly surprised to find recipes of deep fried POORIS and vadas in the Ayurvedic texts, because the popular notion is that rich foods are not recommended in Ayurveda. When we asked Dr. Kalmadi about this, he smiled, "If you maintain a proper, balanced diet as a rule, then these pooris, deep-fried in ghee, will do you no harm occasionally." Yes, balance is the key word, away from the extremes of over indulgence and slimming diets!

1   Steam the grated pumpkin for 5-7 minutes.

2   In a wok, melt the jaggery in 1-2 tbsp water over low flame. Strain to remove scum. Add the steamed pumpkin to the jaggery syrup and cook over low flame for 2 minutes. Transfer to a broad, rimmed dish. When cooled, add the wheat flour, nutmeg, cardamom and salt. Make a firm dough using as little water as required. Knead 1 tsp warm ghee into the dough. Allow to stand covered for 10 minutes.

3   Divide the dough into 10-12 equal portions and roll into balls. Flatten the balls gently between your palms. Since the dough is firm, roll the pooris without dipping into dry flour as in rotis. Instead, apply a dot of ghee on the rolling board to prevent the dough from sticking to it. In case you still find it difficult, dip very lightly in flour as excess flour tends to burn while deep frying. Roll into small discs of 3-4 inch diameter.

4   In a wok, heat ghee for deep frying. Reduce flame and fry the pooris, one or two at a time, turning them over in the hot ghee until golden brown. Remove and place on absorbent paper to rid the pooris of excess ghee.

These pooris with a hint of sweetness taste very nice with Tangy Amti (p.61) and vegetable preparations.

Since these pooris are deep fried, choose a light menu for the rest of the meal. Alternately, avoid deep-frying and roast them on a skillet (refer parathas p.66).

ROTLA WITH MILLETS *pic. on p. 37*

Sorghum flour (jowar) 1 cup
Wheat flour 1 cup

Roti making is an art that can be honed with practice. But making millet bread or ROTLA is the ultimate challenge. Traditionally millet dough is patted between the palms with quick skilful movements and baked over a wood or coal fire. What makes dough of millet flour different from wheat based dough is that it dries as well as breaks very easily. Keeping in mind the nutritional value and delectable flavour of rotlas, here is a more do-able variation using sorghum flour. Sorghum is sweet and astringent in essence. Light, cooling and easy to digest, it is known to be a blood purifier and can be included in your daily diet. It mitigates pitta and kapha, and despite being dry and light, does not aggravate vata when eaten in moderation.

1 In a broad, rimmed dish, mix the sorghum flour and ½ cup wheat flour. Knead into a soft dough by slowly adding warm water. Knead thoroughly. Place the remaining wheat flour beside the dough.

2 Divide the dough into 8-9 equal portions and roll into balls. Flatten one ball between your palms. Now either follow the traditional method of patting the rotla (step 3) or take the easy way out for this one (step 4).

3 **Patting the traditional way**: Sprinkle flour on a rolling board. Dip the flattened dough into some dry flour and with dexterous, circular movements of your palms, pat into a round disc (approx. 5-6 inch diameter). Make sure you do not press down on it too hard, for a little extra pressure will break the dough. With some amount of practice, you will be able to achieve a smooth, even and round rotla, slightly thicker than parathas. If you think this is difficult, remember that traditionally prepared dough of rotla has no wheat in it at all!

4 **Easy way out**: Dip the flattened dough into the dry flour and with a rolling pin, roll into a disc of 5-6 inch diameter, keeping it much thicker than rotis. Dip both sides of the rotla into the dry flour once or twice to make the rolling easier. Each time you do this, dust off all excess flour.

5 Transfer the rotla onto a hot skillet over medium flame. Apply very little water with your palm to lightly dampen the surface, making sure you leave no dry spots. This helps prevent the dough from cracking due to the heat of the flame. Roast for half to one minute before flipping over to roast the second side.

6 With a tong, lift the rotla off the skillet and turn it directly onto the flame. Flip once or twice over flame to ensure even roasting. Do not expect it to puff up like rotis. Roast well over flame to make a crisp rotla.

Serve 1-2 rotlas per person, hot and direct from the fire. Bottle gourd Dal (p.57) or just jaggery makes a tasty accompaniment to these rustic rotlas.

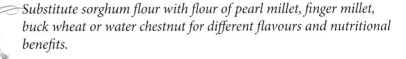
Substitute sorghum flour with flour of pearl millet, finger millet, buck wheat or water chestnut for different flavours and nutritional benefits.

MASALA POORI

Wheat flour 1 heaped cup
Bengal gram flour 1 tbsp
Rice flour 2 tsp
Carom seeds ½ tsp
Fennel seed powder ¼ tsp
Cumin powder ¼ tsp
Turmeric powder ¼ tsp
Red chilli powder 1 tsp
Asafoetida powder a pinch
Mint leaves 2 tbsp, chopped
Coriander leaves 1 tbsp, chopped
Powdered rock salt to taste
Cow's ghee for deep frying

1 Mix all ingredients except ghee in a large, rimmed dish. Make a firm dough using just as much water as required. Allow to stand covered for half an hour.

2 Divide dough into 12-15 balls. Flatten the balls gently between your palms. Since the dough is firm, make the pooris without dipping into dry flour as in rotis. Instead, apply a dot of ghee on the rolling board to prevent the dough from sticking to it. In case you still find it difficult, dip very lightly in flour as excess flour tends to burn while deep frying. Roll into small discs of 3-4 inch diameter.

3 In a wok, heat ghee for deep frying. Reduce flame and fry the pooris, one or two at a time, turning them over in the hot ghee until golden brown. Remove and place on absorbent paper to rid the pooris of excess ghee.

Serve 2-3 hot pooris per person as an evening snack or in a main meal, preferably, lunch.

For the calorie conscious, you can roast these pooris on a skillet (refer parathas p.66) rather than deep-frying.

FENNEL and CAROM, two light and healthy seeds, lend their goodness to this recipe. While fennel is cool, sweet and astringent in essence, carom is hot and sharp with a pungent-bitter essence and pungent post-digestive effect. Both relieve abdominal aches, stimulate digestive fire and are very good for vatas and kaphas. Carom seeds however, tend to increase pitta. This tridoshik recipe has a sprinkling of these seeds in an interesting combination with flours and spices.

SALADS *p.100-101*
Top row left to right: French bean salad, Spiced gooseberry, Beetroot salad, Corn salad
Centre row left to right: Green gram salad, Red pumpkin salad, Leafy salad, Sprout salad, Water chestnut toss
Bottom row left to right: Kohlrabi salad, Mixed salad

JUICES *p.105*
Clockwise from top left: Bottle gourd juice, Apple juice, Kokam juice, Tangy mango juice,
Spinach juice, Gooseberry juice, Ripe mango juice, Sugar sweet cooler

FOOD AND THE MIND *triguna*

Just as the body is governed by the three doshas of vata, pitta and kapha, so also the mind is inclined towards the three modes of sattva, rajas and tamas. Among these, sattva is the state of equlibrium, rajas of action and worldly passion, and tamas of inertia and darkness. There is a constant tug of war between the three, since at a given time, only one can predominate over the others. It is the combination and dynamic interplay of these three modes that gives rise to the notion of the "I" in the human being.

The Bhagavad Gita states that like the mind, food is also of three kinds - sattvik, rajasik and tamasik. If we watch carefully, it can be seen that we are attracted to foods which reflect the mental state we are in. Therefore, we reach out for junk foods when we are under stress and more wholesome foods when in a calm state of mind. However, we have the free will to discipline our minds, to reach out for the right foods at the right time. Such discipline not just in food, but in all aspects of life, can help us shift from a lesser state of mind to a higher state.

SATTVA

Sattva is defined as the state of equlibrium since it endows the individual with nobility in thought, vigilance in action and balance in speech, thus purifying his existence. A person with a sattvik mind is cheerful in all circumstances, detached towards his actions and thereby devoid of pride. Foods that pleasantly satiate the body, leaving it neither overstuffed nor hungry and creating a feeling of lightness and well being are defined as sattvik foods. They are unctuous, sweet, wholesome, nourishing, pleasing to the heart and agreeable to the bodily systems.

Persons in the state of sattva or those who desire to be in such a state are drawn towards sattvik foods. Such foods promote longevity, vitality, strength, health, joy and cheerfulness. They promote the higher qualities in one's life based on individual constitution, such as, comprehension and mental agility in vatas, intelligence and goal orientation in pittas, and calmness and compassion in kaphas.

An example of a sattvik lunch from this collection of recipes would be - broken wheat kheer (p.21), rotla (p.69), home-style pulav (p.75), stuffed pointed gourd (p.45), kokam kadhi (p.56), green gram salad (p.100) and brahmi chutney (p.96), ending with home-style buttermilk (p.102). Sattvik foods are required for those who have chosen a spiritual path in life, who wish to be free of worldly passions and attachments. Making a habit of eating sattvik foods hones the mind to stay in the ideal mode of sattva.

RAJAS

Rajas is defined as the state of action and worldly passion since it is linked with all kinetic processes and activities of the sense organs such as speech, hearing, sight and also physical movements such as walking and running. Rajas is required in order to live a worldly life, since it gives us the energy to be ambitious, goal-oriented and successful. But it also makes us discontent, restless and arrogant.

Foods that leave you feeling overstuffed and unpleasant with a dry, burning sensation in the throat and tongue are defined as rajasik foods. Persons in the state of passion are drawn to rajasik foods. Such foods are excessively bitter, sour, salty, pungent, dry and alkaline.

When eaten in excess, they create physical and emotional imbalances leading to distress, misery and disease. They give rise to indecisiveness and restlessness in vatas, excessive ambition and domination in pittas, and possessiveness for worldly comforts in kaphas. Spicy Indian street foods like chaats, fast foods like pizzas and fries, chillies in excess and parched grains are examples of rajasik foods.

TAMAS

Tamas is defined as the state of inertia and darkness since it is a negative and obstructing energy which pulls us down in life. A person with a tamasik mind is agnostic, ignorant and filled with destructive thoughts, always seeking pleasure through extreme actions. Thus he often finds himself in a state of depression and lethargy, and is prone to addictions.

Foods that cause degeneration in the body, bowel irritation, nausea and related symptoms are defined as tamasik foods. In the state of pale and deathlike darkness, or tamas, one is given to eating foods which smell and taste foul, are under-cooked, half-ripe or overripe, unhygienic, even putrid, stale and impure in extreme situations. They give rise to depression & anxiety in vatas, violence and vengeance in pittas and stubborn sluggishness in kaphas. Eating such foods on a daily basis, contorts the mind and locks it in the state of tamas.

Whether it is inculcating good values and life skills in ourselves and our children, or ensuring excellence of the food we eat, the process of 'preparation', or refinement is very important. This is known as samskara. Ayurvedic texts emphasize the importance of how food should be prepared. Food substances undergo modification, improvement and refinement through the correct process of preparation, thereby making them more beneficial upon consumption.

There is a definite connection between our thoughts and the food we eat. According to the Bhagavad Gita, the relation between our eating and our thinking is of three kinds - we can think before we eat, we can eat before we think, or we can keep the two processes unrelated to each other. A yogi, or a sattvik individual reflects on the consequence of eating a particular food before doing so. A bhogi, or rajasik individual eats first and then thinks. The ignorant one or a tamasik person is interested in eating and disinterested in thinking.

Thus, the seers say, train the mind to be sattvik. Attend to the needs of the body, like hunger and thirst and build a mind that is happy and steadfast. Attending to the hunger of the palette is but a temptation of the unsteady mind that weakens the body and spirit.

It appears to be widely believed that Ayurveda deals only with sattvik and vegetarian food. This is not entirely true. For instance, garlic, ginger and onions, which do not come under sattvik foods, have been praised in Ayurvedic texts for their qualities and medicinal properties. Ayurveda does not ignore the needs of worldly life over yogic endeavour. Nor is it restricted only to the vegetarian population. In fact, many texts are replete with chapters dedicated to the attributes of non-vegetarian foods, their qualities and methods of preparation and consumption. Meats are referred to as 'balakarak' or strengthening. Ayurveda is a way of life that can be adopted by anyone - by those engaged in worldly life, and also by those on the path of spirituality. It is the science of life which gives the formula for happy longevity or sukham ayu for all.

Ayurvedic texts refer to aromatic, long grained rice as the best variety for daily consumption. Categorized as 'shuka dhanya' or grains with pointed ends, this variety of rice is nourishing, unctuous and cooling. It mitigates all the three doshas and hence enjoys a favoured position over other varieties of rice grains. In the new world, basmati rice comes closest to such a description.

The heaviness of freshly harvested rice is reduced when stored for a year under appropriate conditions. Thus, by the influence of time, or 'kala samskara', it undergoes refinement and becomes light and easy to digest.

Spices like cloves, cinnamons, cardamoms and peppercorns are often used in the preparation of rice dishes or pulavs. For those who find these whole spices a hindrance while eating, remember that they can be substituted with a dash of garam masala (refer tip, p.49) as a garnish.

BASIC HOME-STYLE PULAV *pic. on p. 27*

Basmati rice 1 heaped cup
Spinach ½ bunch or 1 heaped cup
Powdered rock salt to taste

The tempering
Cow's ghee 1½ tsp
Bay leaf 1
Cinnamon 2 inch stick
Cloves 2
Cardamoms 2
Cumin seeds 1 tsp

1 Chop spinach and set aside. Wash and soak rice for 10 minutes, strain and set aside.

2 In a pressure pan, heat ghee and add the ingredients of the tempering. When they crackle and let out their aroma, reduce flame and add the chopped spinach, salt and rice. Sauté for 1-2 minutes. Add 2 cups warm water and pressure cook for just 1 whistle.

Allow steam to settle down completely, gently fluff the rice with a fork and serve fresh.

• Substitute spinach with vegetables like beetroot, carrot, cabbage, corn, fenugreek leaves, fresh green peas or any combination that helps balance your dosha (refer food guide p.108).

• When short of vegetables, julienned onions and finely chopped garlic, sautéd in the tempering to light golden, have the capacity to convert this simple home-style pulav into a flavoursome party dish.

• Variation in method: Pulavs can be made in a thick bottomed pan. After adding water in step 3, cook over high flame until the rice comes to a boil. Reduce flame, cover with a rimmed lid and pour ¼ cup water on the lid. This method will require up to 1 extra cup water. Cook until all water evaporates and the rice is done, checking and stirring occasionally. Switch off flame and allow to stand covered with a tight lid for 10-15 minutes.

MINT RICE

Basmati rice 1 heaped cup
Onion 1 medium, julienned
Powdered rock salt to taste

The paste
Mint leaves ½ bunch or ½ cup
Coriander leaves ½ bunch or ½ cup
Fresh coconut ½ cup, grated
Garlic 3-4 cloves
Green chilli 1

The tempering
Cow's ghee 1-2 tsp
Cinnamon 2 inch stick
Cloves 2
Black peppercorns 5
Cumin seeds ½ tsp

1   Wash and soak rice for 10 minutes. Strain and set aside.

2   Grind the ingredients of the paste adding just enough water to make a thick paste.

3   In a pressure pan, heat ghee and add the ingredients of the tempering. When they begin to crackle and let out their aroma, reduce flame and add the onions. Sauté for 4-5 minutes until onions turn light pink. Add the paste and continue to sauté for 2-3 minutes.

4   Add rice, sauté for a minute and add 2 cups warm water along with salt. Pressure cook for just 1 whistle.

Allow steam to settle down completely, gently fluff the rice with a fork and serve fresh.

Another way to make this dish is to cook the rice separately. Now follow steps 2-4 to prepare the masala and stir well along with salt into the cooked rice.

The aromatic MINT leaf is sweet and pungent in essence. It is heavy and has a cooling effect. Said to be good for the heart and for eliminating worms, it balances vata and kapha and stimulates digestive fire. Coriander and coconut lend their sweetness to make this recipe conducive to all doshas.

AROMATIC BIRYANI

Basmati rice 1 heaped cup
Onions 2 medium, julienned
Saffron ¼ tsp
Carrot 1 small, sliced diagonally
Cauliflower 7-8 florets
Shelled double beans ¼ cup
Shelled green peas ¼ cup
Powdered rock salt to taste

The paste
Almonds 6, soaked and peeled
Coriander seeds 1 tsp
Fennel seeds 2 tsp
Poppy seeds 2 tsp
Peppercorns 3-4
Garlic 3-4 cloves
Ginger 2 inch piece
Green chillies 1-2
Coriander leaves ¼ cup
Mint leaves ¼ cup

The tempering
Cow's ghee 1½ tbsp
Bay leaf 1
Cinnamon 2 sticks, 2 inches long
Cloves 3
Black cardamom 2

1   Soak the almonds for 20-30 minutes, peel and grind along with the other ingredients of the paste using very little water.

2   Wash and soak rice for 10 minutes. Strain and set aside.

3   In a pressure pan, heat ghee and add the ingredients of the tempering. When they begin to crackle and let out their aroma, reduce flame and add the onions. Sauté for 4-5 minutes until onions start browning.

4   Add the paste and continue to sauté for 2-3 minutes. Stir in the rice, saffron and vegetables. Add 2 cups warm water along with salt and pressure cook for just 1 whistle.

Allow steam to settle down completely, gently fluff the rice with a fork and serve fresh.

This recipe is an aromatic creation that tastes excellent even without the seemingly indispensable potatoes. It absorbs the rich colour of golden SAFFRON, which is sweet, pungent and bitter in essence. Saffron is light and hot and one of the few spices that balances all doshas. The medley of rice, vegetables, nuts and saffron, exotically spiced in this recipe makes it an ideal preparation for festive occasions.

GODA MASALA PULAV

Basmati rice 1 heaped cup

Onion 1 medium, julienned

Carrot 1 small, sliced diagonally

French beans 5-6, sliced diagonally

Shelled green peas ¼ cup

Yam 7-8 pieces of 1 inch cubes

Goda masala (p.92) 1½ tbsp

Yogurt from cow's milk 1 tbsp, whisked

Grated fresh coconut to garnish

Coriander leaves to garnish

Powdered rock salt to taste

The tempering

Cow's ghee 1 tbsp

Mustard seeds ½ tsp

Caraway seeds 1 tsp

Curry leaves 7-8

Turmeric powder ¼ tsp

Asafoetida powder a pinch

1 Wash and soak the rice for 10 minutes. Strain and set aside.

2 In a pressure pan, heat ghee for tempering. Pop the mustard. Add caraway and when it begins to crackle, reduce flame and add the curry leaves, turmeric and asafoetida.

3 Add onions and sauté for 3-4 minutes. Now add the other vegetables and continue to sauté for 2-3 minutes.

4 Add rice, goda masala, yogurt and salt. Stir well, add 2 cups warm water and pressure cook for just 1 whistle. Allow steam to settle down completely before opening the lid.

Garnish with coconut and chopped coriander leaves. Serve fresh with Kokam Kadhi (p.56) as a delicious accompaniment.

The quickest rice dish to cook-up is one spiced with salt and peppercorns along with CUMIN or CARAWAY seeds, tempered in ghee. These seeds are pungent in essence and lend their aroma to many an Indian delicacy. Although not very heating, they ignite digestive fire. Excellent digestives that aid in relieving nausea, vomiting and diarrhoea, they are also known to improve intelligence, cleanse the uterus, cure fevers and bestow strength. Both cumin and caraway are essential ingredients in the making of Goda masala, which adds its distinctive flavour to this recipe.

SOYA PULAV

Basmati rice 1 heaped cup
Soya chunks ½ cup, minced
Carrot 1 small, sliced diagonally
French beans 5-6, sliced diagonally
Shelled green peas ¼ cup
Turmeric Powder ¼ tsp
Chilli Powder ½ tsp
Lemon juice 1 tsp
Powdered rock salt to taste

The tempering
Cow's ghee 1 tbsp
Bay leaf 1
Cinnamon 2 inch stick
Cloves 2
Cardamom 1-2
Peppercorns 5-6
Cumin seeds ¼ tsp

1 Wash and soak the rice and soya separately for 10 minutes. Strain each and set aside.

2 In a pressure pan, heat ghee and add the ingredients of the tempering. When they crackle and let out their aroma, reduce flame and add the minced soya and vegetables. Sauté for 1-2 minutes before adding the rice.

3 Stir for 2-3 minutes, add turmeric, chilli powder, lemon juice, salt and 2 cups warm water. Pressure cook for just 1 whistle.

Allow steam to settle down completely, gently fluff the rice with a fork and serve fresh.

For a variation in method, steam the rice separately. Prepare the tempering and sauté vegetables and soya in it till well done. Add the remaining ingredients and stir the cooked rice gently into it until well combined.

SOYA leads among legumes in the new world as it is rich in protein content. It is a dicotyledonous seed and thus falls in the category of shimbi dhanya in Ayurveda. Sweet-astringent in essence with a pungent post-digestive effect, legumes are most beneficial when cooked in cow's ghee. Soya beans mitigate pitta and need to be well cooked and spiced for vata and kapha. Ready to cook soya chunks are available in supermarkets world over and are easy to use as in this recipe.

KHICHADI

Split green gram (husked or
unhusked) ½ cup
Basmati Rice ½ cup
Ginger ½ inch piece, grated
Coriander leaves 2 tbsp, chopped
Powdered rock salt to taste

The tempering
Cow's ghee 2 tsp
Cumin seeds ½ tsp
Peppercorns 4-5
Turmeric powder ¼ tsp
Asafoetida powder a pinch

1 Wash rice and gram together in a vessel that will fit into a pressure cooker.

2 In a wok, heat ghee and add the cumin and peppercorns. As they begin to crackle, add the turmeric and asafoetida. When they crackle and let out their aroma, toss this tempering into the rice and gram.

3 Add 4 cups warm water along with ginger, coriander leaves and salt. Pressure cook for 3-4 whistles. This khichadi should be soft and loose in consistency.

A simple, light dinner-time meal.

You may like to add 1 cup mixed, chopped vegetables like beans, carrots, bottle gourd, snake gourd and cauliflower along with the rice for a satisfying single-dish meal.

A popular preparation from ancient times, KHICHADI is an Ayurvedic preparation known as krishara which is made by boiling rice and split lentils together in water, with salt, asafoetida and turmeric. It increases potency, helps in smooth excretion of body waste, is strengthening, heavy and thus most suitable to vatas. Being nutritious and ideal during convalescence, it is also recommended for pittas and kaphas. In this recipe, we have added cooling coriander leaves for pitta and spiked it with peppercorns and ginger for kapha.

LENTIL - BASIL RICE

Basmati rice 1 level cup

Any split lentil (masoor, bengal or red gram) ¼ cup

Basil leaves 2 tbsp, chopped

Onion 1 large, julienned

Ginger 1 tsp, chopped fine

Fennel seeds 1 tbsp, powdered

Poppy seeds 1 tbsp, powdered

Green chilli 1, chopped fine

Powdered rock salt to taste

The tempering

Cow's ghee 1-2 tsp

Bay leaf 1

Cinnamon 2 inch stick

Cloves 3

Cardamom 2

Cumin seeds 1 tsp

1   Wash and soak the rice and lentil together for 10 minutes. Strain and set aside.

2   In a pressure pan, heat the ghee and add the ingredients of the tempering. When they crackle and let out their aroma, add the onions and ginger. Reduce flame and sauté for 3-4 minutes until onions turn light pink.

3   Add the rice, lentil, fennel powder and poppy seed powder. Sauté for 1 minute. Add basil leaves, green chillies and salt along with 2 cups warm water and pressure cook for just 1 whistle.

Allow steam to settle down completely, gently fluff the rice with a fork and serve fresh.

This recipe tastes delicious with moth beans as a substitute for the lentils. Soak for 4-5 hours in warm water and proceed with the recipe. Add ¼ tsp turmeric powder and ¼ tsp chilli powder along with the salt.

ONIONS add flavour to almost any dish with their sweet-pungent essence, their pungency being stronger in the raw state and sweetness enhanced when cooked. Onions are heavy, moist and sharp. Strengthening and aphrodisiacal, they are considered good for all the doshas. However, vatas need to go slow on raw onions and kaphas on cooked ones. Onions, just like ginger and garlic, are not considered sattvik, but are highly respected for their medicinal properties.

EAT WITH AYURVEDIC INSIGHTS *vivekena swaadayet*

Just as thoughts are ignited by the fire of the mind, so also, the food we eat is digested by the fire of the body. Ayurveda describes fire in the human body as being of thirteen kinds, seven related to the seven tissues and five to the five elements. The thirteenth and most vital of them is the digestive fire, or 'jatharagni'. Once food is ingested, this digestive fire leads it systematically through the various stages of digestion, separating waste from necessary nutrients on the way.

When this fire is disturbed or vitiated by poor lifestyles and unhealthy eating habits, the digestive system crashes, leading to the production of 'ama' or toxins in the body, the chief architect of discomfort and disease.

In the context of doshas, vata aggravation leads to irregular metabolism or vishama agni; that of kapha leads to dull metabolism or manda agni and that of pitta leads to sharp metabolism or tikshana agni. Blessed are those who work towards a balanced metabolism or sama agni, for their elements are in perfect balance and their doshas in check. Ayurveda prescribes certain rules for food consumption to ensure that we eat in a way that allows the digestive fire to work well for us.

BEGINNING A MEAL

Every civilization has a tradition of saying a prayer of thanks before a meal. Ayurveda also suggests a mealtime regimen which begins with a prayer for the proper digestion of food and to acknowledge the blessing of food.

Having said your prayer, eat a small quantity of ginger and rock salt before the meal. This stimulates the taste buds so that one can enjoy all the six essences. It also aids in digestion. Start your noon meal with a sweet and avoid it at dinner time for this is heaviest to digest. Then follow it up with rotis, a vegetable, dal and rice. End your noon meal with a glass of buttermilk. Then chew on a teaspoon of roasted fennel seeds or a mouth freshener (p.93) after the meal.

Such a sequence is satiating and enables proper digestion of food, thus giving strength to the body.

FOOD AND HUNGER

Never eat the second meal before the first is digested. Watch for the true signs of digestion which are a feeling of lightness, increased physical energy, excretion of waste products in proper ratio, feeling of thirst and hunger. This would normally result in a 5-6 hour gap between meals. However, do not starve the stomach, and if hungry between meals, eat a fruit or a light snack to see you through to the next meal. When you remain hungry for long, vata increases and the digestive fire of pitta is suppressed, often leading to gastric problems like ulcers and acidity.

May there always be food when you are hungry and water when you are thirsty. For, it is said in Ayurvedic scriptures that hunger must be satiated by food and thirst must be satiated by water. Although this may seem an over-simplified dictum, is it not true that, ever so often, we drink water to kill our hunger, and consume cold drinks to quench our thirst?

WATER

Drinking excess or no water does not help digestion of food. Therefore, to increase the jatharaagni or digestive fire, one must only sip water once or twice in between a meal. Drinking water before a meal leads to weakness, thus dulling the digestive fire. Gulping water at the end of a meal increases kapha, and is a cause for obesity.

So let the children enjoy their little sips of water in between their meals. They seem to know what's good for them by sheer instinct!

FOOD TEMPERATURE AND CHOICE

A meal must include all the six rasas or essences of sweet, sour, salty, bitter, pungent and astringent. Freshly cooked food is ruchikarak, or tasty, ignites the digestive fire, is easily digested, reduces the ill effects of vata such as flatulence, and dries kapha, thereby keeping the body light. So also, food cooked in ghee gives strength to the body and senses, and enhances beauty by lending unctuousness and moisture to those parts of the body which tend to become dry, like skin, joints and eyes. Sesame oil is a good choice for vegans and those who are lactose intolerant.

Food must be consumed at warm temperature because it is meant to accentuate the digestive fire. When it is eaten very hot it kills taste because it has to be gulped down, without proper chewing. This does not help digestion. Food that is cold and dry takes long to digest, and foods with excessive unctuousness cause lack of appetite.

The ancients said that there is no difference between food and medicine. All food can be preventive medicine if consumed in the proper preparation and combination.

AT HOME WITH FOOD

The Ayurvedic scholars advise that one must eat meals in a dear and cherished place of one's home. In such a place, the mind rests and concentrates on the process of eating. It is imperative to proper digestion that one treats mealtimes with respect. In the context of modern life, it is well worth mentioning the unhealthy habit of eating in front of a television. When one eats hurriedly, one tends to swallow rather than chew well. Likewise, eating very slowly is also not advisable because food becomes cold and the post-digestive effect of consumed food goes awry.

Eating in good company, with happy thoughts and complete concentration on food, energizes. Criticizing, worrying or abusing during food consumption depletes you of energy. Even the clothes one wears during cooking, serving and eating should be free of dust, micro-organisms and sweat. Wash your hands and mouth with fresh water before this journey through food preparation and consumption. Last, but not the least, learn to understand your inherent likes and dislikes and your digestive capacity.

The best food is always simple, fresh and home cooked. Cook with love, serve with joy and eat with appreciation so that 'prana' or positive energy passes into the food which nourishes your body.

A balanced constitution is what we must seek through food, because the right balance can help us live healthier and longer lives. Food is meant to gratify and reinforce the body, mind and senses, not to cause uneasiness and distress.

It is probably beyond us to escape the external wrath of the elements in the form of tsunamis, earthquakes, and diseases such as plague, malaria, typhoid and cholera, but by stabilizing our inherent doshas, we can control ailments such as piles, acidity, ulcers, cough, common colds and asthma.

You are what you eat, claims the popular adage. Add to this the knowledge that what you need to eat is not elaborate menus with unavailable and exotic ingredients, but simple home-cooked food using regional and seasonal availables that suit your constitution. This is the quintessence of an Ayurvedic diet in a nutshell.

चतुर्थोऽध्यायः

अथातो रोगानुत्पादनीयमध्यायं व्याख्यास्यामः।
इति ह स्माहुरात्रेयादयो महर्षयः॥

जब गंग में रोगानुत्पादनीय नामक अध्याय की व्याख्या करेंगे। इस निषय में आत्रेय आदि महर्षियों ने इस प्रकार कहा था।

उपक्रम—किस प्रकार का आचरण (आहार-विहार आदि) करने से रोगों की उत्पत्ति न हो अथवा जिस आचरण में कहे जाने वाला विषय रोगों की उत्पत्ति को रोकने के लिए हितकारक हो, उसका नाम है—'रोगानुत्पादनीय' अध्याय। भरत में उक्त आशय से कहे गये अध्याय का नाम है—'योगानुधारणीय'।
(च.सू. २०१७.) इस निषय को भोजनकाल ने इस प्रकार कहा है—'न वेगितोऽन्यकार्यं स्वाधाजलिका साधनासाधनम्'।
पहले जल उत्पन्न वेग का संधारण करे आदि। (पूजन ने अनलनलानु, मल-मूत्र, क्षुधा, अशु, छींक, उद्गार (डकार), नयन, हनिका (हिचक) जे निग आदि के वेग को रोकने पर दूसरे कार्य में कार्य न करे, सबसे पहले उस उत्पन्न वेग का परिशमन करे आदि।
(हैल्डिक 'Gastric') रोग हो जाता है, ऐसा कहा है। ऐसा कहा है—च.सू. २४; च.चि. २१ रामा अ.सं.सू. १ में वेग।

संक्षिप्त सांधेत-संकेत—उ. सू. ०. प.चि. २१ सू.उ. १५ तथा अ.सं.सू. १ में वेग॥

वेगास्‌ धारयेतावामिश्रमश्वतृडुद्गमान्‌। निःश्वासक्षवथुद्गारवातविण्मूत्ररेतसाम्‌॥१ ६॥

वेगों को न रोकने का निर्देश—अपानवायु, मल-मूत्र, छींक, प्यास, भूख, निद्रा, खांसी, बाल, श्रमश्वनित
क्षुधा (संभार), आंसू, वांधि (वमन) तथा शुक्र के वेगों को नहीं रोकना चाहिए॥१ ६॥

व्याख्या—उसी निषय को प्रकृति से भी उत्तरात्मक ५४७-५ में कहा है। भास्नस में तेजी से निःसका
वेग बने रहने पर, रोके जाने के अंनतर भी उसकी भी नित्ति होती है। फलतः 'उदावर्त' रोग की उत्पत्ति हो जाती
जाती रही तथ प्रगट एव निग की भी स्थिति होती है। फलतः 'उदावर्त' रोग की उत्पत्ति हो जाती
जाती है—उधर हटकार कर देने में ना जाने निपरीत किसी अन्य मार्ग से निकल जाता या निग
आवेग न रहकर सका तो उसे अनेक प्रकार की हानियों से हो सकती है। भाव अच
धारयेत्‌।

रोगे ग्रुणोदावर्तिरूक्ष्णा। वातभूयक्लह्यगुष्ठप्रविष्टतुब्वरा॥ २॥

रोकने में हानि—उक्त वेगों को रोकने से गुल्म, उदावर्त, गुल्म तथा क्लम
होता है। अपानवायु, मूत्र तथा पुरीष की वृत्ति में रुकावट आ सकती है॥ २॥

भूयखेला (हुआ का कड़ा आमा) हो सकता है॥ १॥

नेत्ररोग, हृदय में उक्त स्मणे के आद एक यग और इस प्रकार का देखा जाता
इसमें भी प्राय की की स्थिति होती है। आधाप ऐसा लगता ता है कि निग्निम्लारीय इस प्रति को
सरला।

धारयेत्‌। हर्यनले पदिनार्ती हृह्त्यलमुलपद

[page heavily shadowed — right column partially illegible]
भूयमेणेत्रोधन रोग—पुरी
... एकारों का आला ...
... एक एकात्र का आला उपा ...
तैरेण रेग भी हो सकते हैं॥ ...

... रोगों की चिकित्सा
किया जा रहा है—पुरन...
..., होगों अनग्रहण में हो ...

अपान
जिनिकामा-भेद—अन...
... नेत्र में। ...

मूत्रजेन्यु एं ...

मूयखेगरोधज रोग—मूत्र ...
मूयखेगरोधज रोग-चिकित्सा
मूयखेगरोधज रोग के पहले ...
का उस रोके किये गये धूलणात्म से ...

उदारस्याहचि कम्यो निग...
उदारखेगरोधज रोग-चिकित्सा
वा पिका हिका (हिचकी) की नित्ति ...

अज्यम—पाठक ध्यान दें, इस...
... के निपरीत महर्षि ...
भाषा की तो प्राय, भाषा ...
... के अतिरिक्त ...

Evening snack time is commonly observed in India. There is a wide range of healthy, delicious snack preparations ranging from upmas, wadis and cutlets to the popular varieties of Indian pancakes such as dosas of south India and besan chila (pancake of bengal gram flour) of the north. Many of these are popular during breakfast time as well. A variety of lentil and millet flours are available in the markets, including flours of sprouted millets which are useful in making a quick pancake.

Here we begin with a basic home-style pancake made with green gram. Soaked well and made into a delicious batter, this is an excellent tridoshik snack and also helps in recuperation after illness.

BASIC HOME-STYLE CHILA *pic. on p. 37*

Whole green gram 1 cup
Rice 1 tbsp
Ginger 1 inch piece
Garlic 3-4 cloves
Coriander leaves ¼ cup, chopped
Powdered rock salt to taste
Cow's ghee, to drizzle over chila

1 Wash and soak the gram and rice for 3-4 hours. Strain and grind into a smooth batter with the ginger, garlic, coriander leaves and salt, using some of the strained water. The batter should be of thick, pouring consistency.

2 Heat a skillet or non-stick pan and brush with a little ghee. Pour a ladle of the batter on the pan. Spread it as thinly as possible with the base of the ladle into a round and even pancake (chila) of 6-7 inch diameter.

3 Reduce flame and drizzle ¼ tsp ghee (remember to reduce fat for kaphas) around the chila. Allow to cook for 1-2 minutes.

4 When it starts to brown and separates from the pan, flip over with a flat spatula. Cook for 1-2 minutes.

5 Flip again, fold and serve hot.

Serve 1-2 Chilas per person with any chutney from this selection for breakfast.

• *You can add chopped onions, grated carrots, fresh fenugreek leaves and spinach to this batter either singly or in a combination of your choice to enhance taste and nutrition. When using vegetables, roast the pancakes for an extra minute or two.*

DOSA WITH MILLETS

Any millet (sorghum, pearl or
finger millet) 1 heaped cup
Black gram (husked) ¼ cup
Fenugreek seeds 1 tsp
Hibiscus flowers (optional) 10
Powdered rock salt to taste
Cow's ghee, to drizzle over dosa

*MILLETS are categorized as
'kshudra dhanya' or lesser
grains in Ayurveda. They are
generally sweet and astringent
in essence, light, not very
heating, and are said to deplete
body fats. They absorb body
moisture, thus causing dryness
and are binding in nature.
Some of them are prescribed to
aid in the cure of pitta and
kapha ailments. Vatas need to
eat them well cooked in ghee.
The use of black gram also
helps to balance vata.
Traditionally, dosa batter is
allowed to ferment overnight
before consumption. This recipe
deviates from that procedure
since Ayurveda does not
encourage consumption of
fermented foods. It is further
enhanced in nutrition and
texture by the addition of the
beautiful hibiscus flowers
which promote healthy hair
growth and texture.*

1 Wash and soak the millet, gram and fenugreek seeds overnight.

2 Strain the soaked millet mixture and grind into a smooth batter along with hibiscus petals and salt, using some of the strained water. The batter should be of thick, pouring consistency. Set aside for 2-3 hours.

3 Heat a skillet or non-stick pan and brush with a little ghee. Pour a ladle of the batter on the pan. Spread it as thinly as possible with the base of the ladle into a round and even dosa of 6-7 inch diameter.

4 Reduce flame and drizzle ¼ tsp ghee (remember to reduce fat for kaphas) around the dosa. Allow to cook for 1-2 minutes.

5 When it starts to brown and separates from the pan, flip over with a flat spatula. Cook for 1-2 minutes. Flip again, fold and serve hot.

Serve 1-2 dosa per person with Coriander-mint Chutney (p.97) for breakfast.

For a stuffed dosa, we recommend the Yam Stuffing (see variation on p.67). Spread 1 tbsp stuffing on the dosa before folding and serve immediately.

SEMOLINA PANCAKES

Semolina 1 cup
Rice flour (optional) 1 tbsp
Yogurt of cow's milk ½ cup
Onions ½ cup, chopped fine
Carrots or capsicum ¼ cup, grated
or chopped fine
Green chilli 1, chopped fine
Coriander leaves ¼ cup, chopped
Cumin seeds ½ tsp
Asafoetida powder a pinch
Powdered rock salt to taste
Cow's ghee, to drizzle over pancakes

Good for vatas and pittas, SEMOLINA is the refined, grainy form of wheat and carries its sweet, heavy and moist properties. Kaphas, who need to stay light at breakfast, are better off eating wheat and its refined forms during the latter half of the day. This recipe with the use of buttermilk and spices helps reduce the heaviness of semolina.

1 In a wok, dry roast the semolina over low flame for 2-3 minutes.

2 Churn the yogurt with 1 cup water to make buttermilk. Mix the semolina into this buttermilk along with rice flour to make a thick batter of pouring consistency.

3 Mix all other ingredients except ghee into the batter. Allow to stand for 10-15 minutes.

4 Heat a skillet or non-stick pan. Brush the pan with a little ghee. Pour a ladle of the batter on the pan. Spread it with the base of the ladle into a slightly thick round pancake approx. 5-6 inches in diameter.

5 Reduce flame and drizzle ¼ tsp ghee for vatas and pittas and just a few drops for kaphas around the pancake. Cover and allow to cook for 1-2 minutes. Remove cover.

6 When it starts to brown and separates from the pan, flip over with a flat spatula. Cook for 2-3 minutes.

Serve 1-2 pancakes per person with any chutney from this selection for breakfast.

Add ½ cup vermicelli and reduce the quantity of semolina accordingly. Roast the pancakes for an extra 2-3 minutes.

BROKEN WHEAT UPMA

Broken wheat 1 cup
Onions 2, chopped fine
Green chillies 1-2, chopped fine
Coriander leaves 2 tbsp
Lemon juice 2 tsp, freshly squeezed
Powdered rock salt to taste

The tempering
Cow's ghee 2 tsp
Split black gram (husked) 1 tsp
Mustard seeds ½ tsp
Asafoetida powder a pinch
Curry leaves 4-6

1 In a wok, heat ghee for tempering. Add the black gram and as it turns golden, pop the mustard. With the spluttering of the mustard, reduce flame and add the asafoetida and curry leaves.

2 Immediately, add the onions and chillies to this tempering and sauté over low flame for 2-3 minutes. Now add the broken wheat and continue to sauté for 3-4 minutes.

3 Alongside, bring to boil 2 cups water in a pan. When it starts boiling, pour gently but swiftly into the broken wheat, stirring all the while. Add salt and continue to stir until all the water evaporates and the upma begins to leave the sides of the wok.

4 Switch off flame and allow to stand covered for 5-7 minutes. Add lemon juice and coriander leaves and gently fluff up the upma.

Serve as a fresh wholesome breakfast or a light dinner.

*"Caught in the midst of two stones working in opposite directions, nothing remains whole or intact." Reminding us of life's duality and transitory nature, the great poet Kabir wrote this couplet while reflecting on the action of the grinding stone as it ruthlessly broke WHEAT into its granular forms and finally into fine flour. On its own, wheat is cold in potency, sweet in essence, heavy and moist. In this recipe, broken wheat undergoes **agni samskara** or 'refinement by fire' by being roasted, thus becoming light to digest.*

You may like to experiment with this recipe by adding soya chunks to it. Chop 5-6 chunks into bite-size pieces, wash and add to the boiling water in step 3. Likewise, sauté a few ½ inch cubes of tofu and add along with the coriander leaves in step 4. A fistful of finely chopped and boiled vegetables like carrots and french beans or green peas is a welcome and nutritious addition to this preparation.

Rava Upma: Follow the same recipe to make the popular Indian snack using semolina instead of broken wheat. Add 1 cup extra water to make a soft upma as semolina absorbs more water.

Vermicelli Upma: Substitute broken wheat with 1 cup vermicelli and follow the recipe.

BEATEN RICE UPMA

Beaten rice (medium variety) 2 cups
Split green gram (husked) 2 tbsp
Shelled green peas ¼ cup, boiled
Onion 1, chopped fine
Ginger 1 inch piece, grated
Fresh lemon juice 1 tbsp
Coriander leaves to garnish
Powdered rock salt to taste

The tempering
Cow's ghee 2 tsp
Mustard seeds 1 tsp
Cumin seeds 1 tsp
Roasted groundnuts 1 tbsp
Asafoetida powder a pinch
Turmeric powder a pinch
Green chillies 1-2, chopped fine
Curry leaves 5-6

1   Cook the green gram until soft, but make sure it remains whole. Strain and set aside.

2   Rinse the beaten rice. Unlike rice, this does not need to soak nor cook in much water. Rinse just once, but quickly, gently and thoroughly. Squeeze out water and spread lightly on a flat tray for 15-20 minutes till it becomes fluffy and ready to cook. Sprinkle a little water once or twice to keep it soft.

3   In a wok, heat ghee for tempering. Pop the mustard and add the cumin. As it begins to crackle, reduce flame and add remaining ingredients of the tempering.

4   Add the onions and ginger and sauté until onions turn light pink. Now add the beaten rice, cooked gram and boiled peas. Stir gently until well combined.

5   Switch off flame and allow to stand covered with a tight lid for 5-7 minutes. Remove lid, add the lemon juice and chopped coriander leaves.

Serve fresh for breakfast or as a light dinner with Coriander-mint Chutney (p.97).

ASAFOETIDA is pungent, hot, dry and sharp, and mitigates vata and kapha. TURMERIC is bitter, pungent, astringent, hot, dry and light, and balances all the doshas. Both are pungent after digestion and stimulate the digestive fire. They are much used in Indian cooking, as in this snack made with BEATEN RICE which is quick to digest and good for all doshas. Ensure the beaten rice is of medium variety. If too fine, it will become a mash and if too thick, it will not soften easily.

CORIANDER WADI

Coriander leaves 3 cups, chopped
Bengal gram flour 1 cup
Rice flour 1 tbsp
Coriander powder 1 tsp
Cumin powder 1 tsp
Red chilli powder ½ tsp
Powdered rock salt to taste
Cow's ghee 1 tbsp

The tempering
Mustard seeds ½ tsp
Sesame seeds ½ tsp
Carom seeds ½ tsp
Asafoetida powder a pinch
Curry leaves 4-5

1 Mix the coriander leaves, flours, spice powders, salt and 1 tsp warm ghee. Knead into a soft dough adding just as much water as required. Divide this dough into 4-5 portions.

2 Grease your palms with a little ghee and roll each portion into 2 inch thick cylindrical shapes. Place these long rolls in a vessel that fits in a pressure cooker. Steam without the whistle for 10 minutes.

3 Cool the rolls and chop into bite-sized pieces, approx. ½ inch thick.

4 In a wok, heat the remaining ghee for tempering. Pop the mustard and add the sesame and carom seeds. As they start crackling, add the asafoetida and curry leaves. Toss the wadis into this tempering and switch off flame.

Serve a modest portion of wadis per person as a tea time snack.

Vatas must eat this snack sparingly since bengal gram aggravates vata. You can also reduce bengal gram flour to ½ cup and add green gram flour since it is tridoshik and more nutritious.

Indispensable in Indian cooking, the CORIANDER leaf displays sweet and astringent rasas. With its sweet post-digestive effect, it enhances digestive fire and reduces excessive thirst and body heat. It is a diuretic and helps relieve nausea, piles, asthma and cough. No wonder then, that this light, moist and refreshing herb is so coveted that in areas where it is available only seasonally, its leaves are dried and used for the rest of the year. It is a tridoshik herb, good for all when dried and especially good for pitta when fresh.

YAM CUTLET

Yam 200 gms (1½ cups when chopped)
Onion 1 small, chopped fine
Beetroot ¼ cup, peeled and grated
Carrot ¼ cup, peeled and grated
French beans 4-5, chopped fine
Shelled green peas ½ cup
Ginger garlic paste 1 tsp
Green chillies 1-2, chopped fine
Coriander leaves ¼ cup, chopped
Turmeric powder ¼ tsp
Garam masala (refer tip, p. 49) ½ tsp
Powdered rock salt to taste
Semolina (fine variety) ½ cup
Cow's ghee to drizzle over cutlets

1 Peel, wash and chop the yam into medium chunks. Boil along with turmeric in a pan of water. When soft, strain, mash and set aside.

2 Boil the chopped beans and peas. Strain.

3 Squeeze out water from grated beetroot and carrot.

4 Mix all the ingredients together except semolina and ghee. Divide into 8-10 lemon sized balls. Now press them between your palms into round or oval shaped flat cutlets about ¾ inch thick.

5 Spread the semolina on a broad, flat tray and dip each cutlet into it, making sure they are well coated on all sides.

6 Heat a skillet coated with ghee. Shallow fry the cutlets by drizzling a little ghee around them two or three times until dark golden on both sides.

Serve 1-2 cutlets per person with Spinach Chutney (p.99) or Coriander-mint Chutney (p.97).

> The dry and light YAM provides an excellent substitute to potatoes as in this recipe. It enhances digestive fire, is astringent and pungent, and works as a cure for abdominal tumours, enlarged spleen and piles. Considered best among root vegetables, it can be eaten regularly by vatas and kaphas. Its pungency can be handled by pittas only in moderation. Beans, peas and coriander leaves provide a good balance in this recipe. The use of semolina instead of the commonly used bread crumbs for coating the cutlets is a further health addition in this snack. Wash the yam very well and cook with a pinch of turmeric to avoid irritation and itching in the throat.

A READY KITCHEN *gunayuktam mahanasam*

A shloka from Kshema Kutuhalam *says, "A kitchen should be equipped with essential ingredients which are cleaned and stored appropriately; with a cook who is vigilant and active; sprinkled with substances that repel insects and worms; and exuding a pleasant fragrance. It should be well ventilated and ideally located in the South-east corner."*

Ayurveda prescribes the use of certain utensils for cooking and serving food such as earthenware, stone, iron and wood. Mention is also made of gold and silver utensils as being very good for cooking purposes as they help increase intelligence and mitigate all doshas. Copper must be avoided as a cooking utensil as it has the quality of sourness which increases pitta. However foods that are not sour can be served in copper utensils, once cooked.

Some basic essentials to enjoy an Ayurvedic experience with this book in your kitchen are - the Indian spice box, a pestle and mortar, mixie, rolling board and pin, skillet and tongs, buttermilk churner, and of course, the pressure cooker with its deafening sound in the wee hours of the morning and evenings too. Other indispensables are cow's ghee, fresh yogurt, rock sugar and rock salt. Chunks of ROCK SUGAR (pic. on p.110) are available in almost all Indian grocery stores and light pink blocks of ROCK SALT (pic. on p.110) are available at Ayurvedic outlets, both of which can be powdered at home, and are much recommended. Also included in this chapter are a few interesting recipes that can be made in advance and preserved.

SPICE BOX *pic. on p.111*

Not a day in an Indian household goes by without the delicious aroma of tempering, except when a family is in mourning, at which time no food is cooked at all. A simple popping of mustard, cumin and asafoetida along with other spices can enhance the flavour of almost any dish, starting from simple salads to exotic biryanis. Every region, every community, even every family for that matter, has its own distinctive style of tempering with the common factor being the ever handy spice box.

Tempering is a quick process, leaving no time to open containers one after the other. Thus, keeping the basic ingredients together in the spice box is a practical solution.

Typically the box has seven compartments. The ingredients that go into them are: cumin, split black gram, mustard, chilli powder, turmeric powder and coriander powder. The seventh container in the centre is filled with cinnamon, cloves and cardamom. A tiny bottle of asafoetida powder can be placed along with the mustard. The box is fitted with a rimmed tray for dry red chillies and bay leaves.

GODA MASALA

We include this masala as a tribute to the hills of Maharashtra where KARE, our inspirational space, is nestled. Goda masala is used to spice up vegetables, dals, rice dishes and khichadis.

Dry roast ¼ cup sesame seeds and ½ cup grated dry coconut, each separately over low flame until golden brown. Set aside.

Heat 1 tbsp ghee and add 1 tbsp cloves, 4 sticks cinnamon, 3 bay leaves, 2 tbsp cumin seeds, 1 tsp black cumin seeds and ¼ tsp fenugreek seeds. When they begin to crackle, add 2 cups coriander seeds and 25-30 dry red chillies. Roast on a low flame until the coriander seeds turn light brown. Add 1 tbsp asafoetida powder and ½ tsp turmeric, roast for 1-2 minutes and switch off flame.

Grind all the ingredients into a fine powder. You may pound the roasted sesame separately with a pestle and mortar, to avoid it turning pasty and add to the ground powder at the end. Store in an air tight container.

Use the shrivelled variety of red chilli (local Maharashtrian name: Bagri Mirchi) to get the traditional dark brown, almost blackish colour of this very unique spice powder.

COW'S GHEE

Ayurveda prescribes the use of *ghritam* or ghee (clarified butter) made from cow's milk for its nourishing qualities. Ghee is sweet, promotes digestion, enhances memory and longevity, is used as an eye and laryngeal tonic, and leaves you with glowing, beautiful skin. It balances all the doshas.

To prepare cow's ghee, use 1-2 kgs of white butter (readily available in grocery stores) churned from cow's milk. In a large pan, melt the butter over medium flame. Reduce flame and continue to simmer, stirring occasionally until all water evaporates and the clear liquid ghee is formed. You will now see clear bubbles on the surface and a golden brown residue at the bottom of the wok. Switch off flame and immediately add a fistful of holy basil or curry leaves to enhance aroma. Allow to become warm, strain and store in a cool, dry place. When cooled it is yellowish in colour because of the carotene pigment it contains. Well made ghee can stay fresh for months.

YOGURT

Yogurt made from cow's milk is nourishing, strengthening and lighter than yogurt made from other milks. It is sweet-sour in essence, hot in potency, enhances taste and kindles digestive fire. According to Ayurveda, the most beneficial way to consume yogurt is in its churned and diluted form called takra or buttermilk.

To make yogurt, boil 2 cups of cow's milk, pour into a bowl and set aside. When lukewarm, vigorously stir in 1 teaspoon of yogurt culture until the milk froths up a bit. Cover and set aside in a warm corner of your kitchen.

In warm climates, it takes 8-10 hrs for yogurt to set. In cold climates, try placing the bowl of warm milk (with the culture) inside a casserole overnight. A unique innovation we discovered at a cold hill station, is to place a whole green chilli in the milk along with the culture. Once set, the chilli can be discarded.

LEMON PICKLE

Wash 10-15 lemons and place them in a bottle along with as much rock salt crystals (almost ½ kg) required to cover the lemons. Keep closed and shake twice a day, for 10-15 minutes. Once in a few days, leave the bottle turned upside down to ensure all the lemons are evenly coated with salt. After 2-3 weeks, when the lemons have turned brown and soft, transfer them into a colander.

Wash them quickly under running water to remove excess salt. Wipe dry with a clean cloth and preserve in a jar. These delicious and healthy lemons can be preserved for months and included in daily meals.

POST-MEAL DIGESTIVE

In a wok, dry roast 1 cup fennel seeds and ¼ cup carom seeds over low flame for 8-10 minutes or until their aromas rise. Grind into a coarse powder. Add 1½ tbsp liquorice powder and 1 tsp cardamom powder. Mix well and store in an air tight container. Chewing a teaspoonful after meals brings about satiation and aids digestion.

Be vigilant while buying and storing ingredients. Buy items that are infrequently used in small quantities. Check vegetables for freshness; cauliflowers, lady's finger and greens, especially for worms; and flours, grains and semolina for insects.

Use these simple tips to ensure your groceries do not spoil:

Clean ingredients as and when you buy them and store them in dry containers.

Parad tablets, available in Indian pharmacies, help keep away worms and insects when placed along with stored grains.

Neem leaves make an organic alternative to Parad tablets in rice containers.

Roast semolina before storing and do not store millet flours for more than a week.

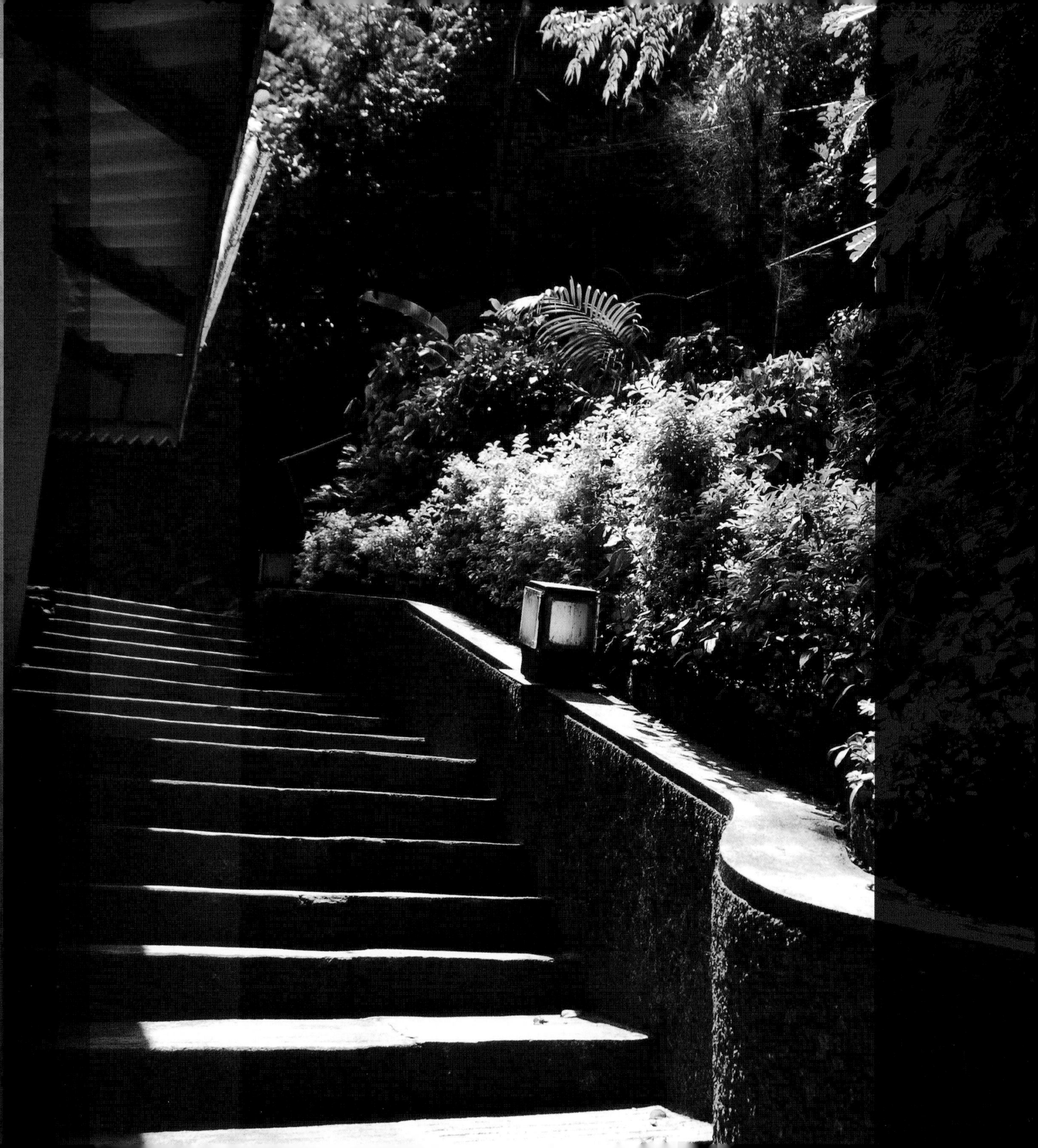

The state of Andhra Pradesh is famous for its chutneys, known as Pachchadi. To be mixed into rice and eaten, all you have to do is sauté almost any vegetable in an aromatic tempering and grind into a chutney. We start this section with a home-style chutney using ridge gourd in a tridoshik combination with spices. Cold in potency and sweet in essence, ridge gourd mitigates pitta and stimulates digestive fire. Although it increases vata and also kapha to some extent, it is said to be an effective remedy for worms, fevers, common cold, cough and fatigue.

With regard to salads and juices in this section, Ayurveda recommends that one should not consume raw foods. Processes like steaming, churning, grinding, boiling or baking help food substances undergo **agni samskara** or refinement by fire. This improves the quality of food, and also helps reduce microbial load present in raw foods. However, onions, and herbs such as mint, parsley, celery, basil and coriander, can be used raw, but in lesser quantities.

HOME-STYLE CHUTNEY *pic. on p. 37*

Tender ridge gourd 1
Fresh coconut 1 tbsp, grated
Thick tamarind pulp 1 tbsp
Coriander leaves 2 tbsp
Powdered rock salt to taste
Cow's ghee 1-2 tsp

The tempering
Split black gram 1 tbsp
Mustard seeds 1 tsp
Cumin seeds 1 tsp
Asafoetida powder ¼ tsp
Dry red chilli 1
Green chilli 1
Curry leaves 6-8

1   Nick off the ends of the ridge gourd, scrape only the rough outer skin and chop into chunks. This should amount to 1 cup.

2   In a wok heat ½ tsp ghee. Add ridge gourd and sauté for 2-3 minutes. Transfer to a bowl and set aside.

3   In the same wok, heat the remaining ghee for tempering. Add the gram and as it turns golden, pop the mustard and cumin. Reduce flame and add asafoetida, chillies and curry leaves.

4   Cool and grind the tempering along with coconut, tamarind pulp, coriander leaves and salt into a paste. Now add the ridge gourd and grind coarsely.

Serve as a lip-smacking accompaniment to a meal, or simply enjoy with steamed rice.

• *Substitute ridge gourd with chayote squash, ivy gourds, onions, raw mangoes (with a dash of jaggery), curry leaves or any greens of your choice.*

BRAHMI CHUTNEY

Brahmi leaves 1 bunch
Coriander leaves 1 cup
Green chillies 1-2
Fresh coconut 1 tbsp, grated
Powdered rock salt ¼ tsp

The tempering
Cow's ghee 1 tsp
Cumin seeds ¼ tsp
Coriander seeds ½ tsp
Asafoetida powder ¼ tsp

1 Discard the stems and wash the brahmi leaves well. This should amount to 1 cup.

2 In a wok, heat ghee for tempering. Add cumin and coriander seeds. When they begin to crackle, reduce flame and add asafoetida powder.

3 Immediately add the brahmi, coriander leaves and green chillies. Sauté for a few seconds. Switch off flame.

4 Cool and grind into a coarse chutney along with coconut and salt.

Serve fresh as an accompaniment in a meal.

Substitute brahmi leaves with fresh curry leaves for a distinctive change in flavour. The curry leaf, which is grown in almost every Indian home, is aromatic and known for its medicinal benefits. Add a dash of tamarind pulp and jaggery when you make this chutney with curry leaves.

The BRAHMI leaf is bitter, astringent and sweet. Light and cooling, this medicinal herb is described as medhya rasayani which means it increases grasping power and memory. It is also known to strengthen immunity and is good for all doshas.

CORIANDER - MINT CHUTNEY

Coriander leaves 2 cups

Mint leaves 1 cup

Brahmi leaves (or spinach) ¼ cup

Almonds 6-8

Raisins 8-10

Large Indian gooseberries 2, grated

Green chillies 1-2

Cumin seeds 1 tsp

Powdered rock salt to taste

Cow's ghee 1 tsp

1 Soak the almonds and raisins for 10-15 minutes. Peel the almonds. and set aside.

2 Discard the stems and wash the coriander, mint and brahmi leaves well. Drain out all water and sauté in ghee for just a minute. Add the grated gooseberries and switch off flame.

3 Grind along with the remaining ingredients, including almonds and raisins, into a paste using 1-2 tbsp water.

Serve as a healthy accompaniment in a meal or as a dip with Chila (p.85) and Cutlet (p.91).

*RAISINS are sweet and cool, and mitigate vata and pitta. When soaked, they can also be eaten by kaphas in moderation. In this recipe, raisins are added to give a hint of sweetness. The Indian GOOSEBERRY or **amla** is known as **dhatriphala** meaning 'mother fruit'. Endowed with the goodness of five rasas, it nourishes all doshas. This aphrodisiac possesses rich medicinal value and is especially useful in controlling bleeding disorders and diabetes. Drinking a small quantity of amla juice everyday keeps body and mind healthy. This chutney is enhanced with gooseberries, the richness of almonds and raisins, and the much recommended Brahmi leaf.*

A popular Indian preparation, the coriander-mint chutney is a choice accompaniment to snacks and meals. If you cannot procure gooseberry, add 1 tbsp grated raw mango or 1 tsp freshly squeezed lemon juice.

CARROT CHUTNEY

Carrot 1
Coriander seeds 2 tsp
Sesame seeds 2 tsp
Dry red chillies 2
Thick tamarind pulp 1 tbsp
Powdered rock salt to taste

The tempering
Cow's ghee 1 tsp
Split black gram 1 tsp
Mustard seeds ½ tsp
Cumin seeds ½ tsp
Dry red chilli 1, nicked at tail
Asafoetida powder a pinch
Curry leaves 4-5

1 Peel and chop the carrot into chunks. Steam for 5 minutes. Set aside to cool.

2 Dry roast coriander seeds, sesame and red chillies for 2-3 minutes over low flame until they turn light brown. Switch off flame and grind into a fine powder.

3 Grind the steamed carrot, tamarind and salt along with the coriander-sesame powder into a paste. There is no need to add water since steamed carrots are juicy enough. Transfer to a bowl.

4 For the tempering, heat ghee in a small wok and add the gram. Stir and as the gram turns golden, add the mustard and then the cumin. Reduce flame and with the crackling of the cumin, switch off flame and add the red chilli, asafoetida and curry leaves. Garnish the carrot chutney with this crunchy tempering.

Serve as a delectable accompaniment in a meal.

Tempering needs practice and a love for detail as Pedatha taught us during the making of our first book. Make sure that the right temperature of ghee is maintained so that ingredients neither burn nor remain undercooked. In a good TEMPERING, the gram turns rose-red, mustard and cumin spread their crackling aromas, and red chillies turn bright red without browning. These simple guidelines are a promise of good taste and healthy benefits.

SPINACH CHUTNEY

Spinach 1 small bunch or 2 cups
Brahmi or coriander leaves ½ cup
Black peppercorns 6-7
Cumin seeds ½ tsp
Green chilli 1
Coconut 1 tbsp, grated
Yogurt of cow's milk 1-2 tbsp
Powdered rock salt to taste
Cow's ghee 1-2 tsp

The tempering
Split black gram ½ tsp
Mustard seeds ½ tsp
Asafoetida powder a pinch
Curry leaves 3-4

1 In a wok, heat ½ tsp ghee and add the peppercorns and cumin. As they start popping, add the spinach, brahmi and green chilli. Sauté for 1-2 minutes.

2 Grind into a fine paste along with coconut and salt without adding any water. Add the yogurt and mix well.

3 For the tempering, heat ghee in a small wok and add the gram. Stir, add the gram and as it turns golden, pop the mustard. Switch off flame and add the asafoetida and curry leaves. Immediately garnish the spinach chutney with this crunchy tempering.

Serve with steamed rice or as a tasty meal accompaniment.

This recipe has the consistency of a dip rather than a chutney because of the addition of yogurt. You could experiment with other greens as well.

The SPINACH leaf is said to be a blood purifier and relieves intoxication. However, it often causes discomfort and flatulence in vatas, thus it is not much recommended for them as part of their daily food. This dry, cooling leaf is more beneficial to pittas and kaphas with its sweet and astringent essence. It gives of its best when boiled or cooked well in a little ghee, thus making it moderately suitable for vatas too.

SALAD SPREAD *pic. on p.71*

CORN SALAD

Steam 1 cup tender corn kernels.

Finely chop the petals of 3 hibiscus flowers, 1 small carrot and ½ capsicum. Sauté together in a dot of ghee for 10-15 seconds. Cool.

Toss all the above ingredients along with 1 tbsp chopped coriander and mint leaves. Season with salt and pepper and serve fresh.

SPICED GOOSEBERRY

Wash and steam 10-12 large Indian gooseberries for 5-7 minutes. Cut along their striations and remove seeds. Add salt and a dash each of chilli powder, turmeric and mustard powder. Set aside.

Heat 1 tsp ghee, add ¼ tsp each of fenugreek, nigella and fennel seeds. Allow to crackle, add a dash of asafoetida powder, toss in the gooseberries and switch off flame. Serve as an accompaniment in a meal.

BEETROOT SALAD

Peel and steam 1 beetroot for 4-5 minutes. Remove liquid, cool, grate and set aside.

Finely chop the petals of 3 hibiscus flowers and 1 small onion. Sauté in ½ tsp ghee for a few seconds. Mix into the beetroot. Add a few pieces of finely chopped green chilli, 1 tbsp chopped coriander leaves, 2 tbsp yogurt and salt to taste.

Garnish with the crunch of black gram, mustard, asafoetida and curry leaves tempered in 1 tsp ghee. Serve fresh.

You may substitute beetroot with tender red radish.

All salads must be prepared 5-10 minutes before serving. It is a good practice to give agni samskara or 'REFINEMENT BY FIRE' to all raw vegetables even if just for a minute. So blanch or sauté the vegetables in your salad to make them lighter for digestion. Dr. Roli at KARE always advises that even salads must be consumed only in moderation, just as everything else. All salads below serve four by the Ayurvedic norm of moderation.

FRENCH BEAN SALAD

Steam 1 cup thin, diagonal strips of french beans for 3-4 minutes.

Finely chop ½ capsicum and 1 small carrot. Sauté together for 1 minute in a dot of ghee.

Cool the vegetables and toss them all together along with 1-2 tbsp fresh pomegranate and chopped coriander leaves. Season with salt and pepper. Serve fresh.

GREEN GRAM SALAD

Wash and soak ¾ cup split green gram (husked) for 3-4 hours. Strain and set aside.

Blanch 3 medium-sized carrots, peel and grate.

Toss the soaked gram and carrots along with 3-4 finely chopped dates, a few pieces of finely chopped green chilli, a dash of lemon juice, chopped coriander leaves and salt to taste.

Garnish with the crunch of black gram, mustard and asafoetida tempered in 1 tsp ghee. Serve fresh.

KOHLRABI SALAD

Steam 1 cup bite-sized cubes of kohlrabi for 4-5 minutes. Strain and set aside to cool.

Sauté ¼ cup chopped spring onion leaves in a dot of ghee for a few seconds. Mix into the kohlrabi and allow to cool.

Add a few pieces of finely chopped green chilli, 1 tbsp chopped coriander leaves, 2 tbsp whisked yogurt.

Garnish with the crunch of black gram, mustard, asafoetida and curry leaves tempered in 1 tsp ghee. Season with salt and serve fresh.

SPROUT SALAD

Steam 2 cups green gram sprouts (refer tip, p.42) for 5-7 minutes.

Finely chop ½ capsicum and 1 small onion. Sauté together for 1 minute in a dot of ghee. Toss into the sprouts and set aside to cool.

Add 1-2 tsp finely chopped apples, coriander and mint leaves. Season with salt and a dash of lemon juice. Serve fresh.

RED PUMPKIN SALAD

Steam 1 cup bite-sized cubes of red pumpkin for 4-5 minutes until well cooked, but crunchy. Strain and set aside to cool.

Finely chop 1 small onion, ½ green chilli and 1 tbsp coriander leaves and mix into the pumpkin along with 2 tbsp whisked yogurt.

Garnish with the crunch of black gram, mustard, asafoetida and curry leaves tempered in 1 tsp ghee. Season with salt and serve fresh.

MIXED SALAD

Steam together ½ cup each of finely chopped french beans, carrots and radish for 2-3 minutes. Allow to cool.

Finely chop 1 small onion, ½ green chilli and 1-2 lettuce leaves and add to the steamed vegetables along with a dash of black salt.

Stir in 2 tbsp whisked yogurt and serve fresh.

WATER CHESTNUT TOSS

Wash, peel and slice ¼ kg tender water chestnuts.

Sauté for 1-2 minutes in 1 tsp ghee. Season with salt and pepper. Add a dash of lemon juice, garnish with coriander leaves and serve fresh.

LEAFY SALAD

Steam 3 cups shredded lettuce or spinach without adding any water for 2 minutes. Alternately, blanch by putting into hot water and strain immediately. Set aside to cool.

Finely chop 1 small onion and 1 small carrot. Sauté together for 1 minute in a dot of ghee.

Cool the vegetables and toss them all together along with 1 tbsp crunchy groundnut powder, a fistful of chopped celery leaves, 1 tsp lemon juice and ½ tsp honey.

Season with salt and pepper. Serve fresh.

HOME-STYLE BUTTERMILK

Fresh yogurt of cow's milk 1 cup
Roasted cumin powder ¼ tsp
Powdered rock salt to taste
Coriander or mint leaves to garnish

The tempering (optional)
Ghee ¼ tsp
Mustard seeds ¼ tsp
Asafoetida powder a pinch
Ginger ¼ tsp, grated

1 Combine yogurt and 3 cups drinking water and churn with a traditional wooden churner or a hand blender until a light froth appears on top.

2 Add roasted cumin powder and salt. Garnish with chopped coriander or mint leaves.

3 If you like tempered buttermilk, heat the ghee for tempering in a wok.

4 Add the mustard and as it begins to splutter, add the asafoetida powder and grated ginger. Pour this tempering into the buttermilk.

Serve 1 cup per person towards the end of lunch.

*After meal drinks are known as ANUPANA in Ayurvedic texts. Buttermilk or **takra**, which is diluted and churned yogurt, is considered an ideal anupana after lunch. There is often a misconception that yogurt and buttermilk have similar properties. According to Ayurveda, yogurt which is hot and sour in essence, when churned into buttermilk, undergoes manthan samskara and becomes sweet after digestion, and exerts a cooling effect. The sutras proclaim, "Just as nectar is for Gods, buttermilk is for humans. One who consumes buttermilk daily does not suffer from disease and diseases cured by it do not recur."*

SPICED BUTTERMILK

Fresh yogurt of cow's milk 2 cups
Powdered rock salt to taste
Cow's ghee 1 tsp

The paste
Cumin seeds ½ tsp
Black peppercorns 3-4
Spinach 6-8 large leaves
Fresh hibiscus petals (optional) 10
Fresh coconut 1 tbsp, grated

The tempering
Cumin seeds ½ tsp
Asafoetida powder a pinch
Curry leaves 4-5, chopped fine

1 Churn yogurt along with 1½ cups water to make buttermilk. Add salt and set aside.

2 For the paste, heat ½ tsp ghee in a wok. Add cumin and pepper and as they crackle, toss in the spinach and hibiscus and sauté for 1-2 minutes. Cool and grind into a fine paste along with the coconut and ¼ cup water. Strain this paste into the buttermilk.

3 For the tempering, heat ½ tsp ghee in the same wok. Add cumin and as it crackles, add the asafoetida and curry leaves. Immediately switch off flame and pour this tempering into the buttermilk.

Serve as a post lunch drink or as an accompaniment to steamed rice.

This drink can be made using leaves of brahmi, coriander, mint or sunberry instead of spinach.

BUTTERMILK kindles the digestive fire, bestows nourishment and is an aphrodisiac. Its light and water absorbent properties make it useful in controlling diarrhoea and dysentery. Its sour essence and warming potency, coupled with the fact that it is a good appetizer and digestive makes it soothing to vatas. Its astringent essence coupled with it being dry, light and quick to digest, calms kapha; and its sweet post-digestive effect keeps it from aggravating pitta. Enjoy this 'thambli', a popular buttermilk from Karnataka.

SPICE TEA

The spice tea mixture

Dried ginger ½ cup when pounded

Peppercorns ½ cup

Coriander seeds ½ cup

Fennel seeds ½ cup

Cloves 5-6

Cardamom 12-15, with pod

While making tea

Cow's milk ¼ cup

Powdered rock sugar 1-2 tsp

1 Mix all the ingredients of the spice tea mixture and grind to a fine powder. Fill into an airtight container and store in a cool place.

2 To make 1 cup tea, boil 1 tsp of the spice tea powder in 1 cup water for 7-8 minutes on medium flame.

3 Switch off flame, strain and pour into a cup.

4 Stir in ¼ cup hot milk along with sugar.

Drink hot, not more than one cup a day.

DRIED GINGER is light and moist, pungent in essence and sweet in post-digestive effect. It is an excellent digestive and relieves constipation. PEPPER stimulates appetite with its sharp, warming effect. Dry and pungent in essence and post-digestive effect, it balances vata and kapha. It does not increase pitta when consumed in moderation. The pungency and sharpness of ginger and pepper is well balanced in this recipe with the cooling coriander and fennel seeds. Both are sweet after digestion. CORIANDER is diuretic, easily digestible, mitigates nausea, burning sensation and all the doshas. FENNEL increases pitta when taken in excess. Tea made from these spices is invigorating, sharp-sweet and a sure reliever of common cold and cough.

You can add a few leaves of mint or a few strips of lemon grass leaves while boiling the tea for a healthy variation and different flavour. An ideal tea for vatas, reduce the milk to counteract its heaviness for kaphas. For pittas, reduce quantity of spice mixture and add a few dried rose petals to the boiling tea.

To make HERBAL TEA, boil a dash of any herb or spice in one cup water over low flame for 5-6 minutes. Strain and serve hot. Check the list of 'herbal teas' in food guide (p.109) to know which teas are suitable to you.

FRUIT AND VEGETABLE JUICES *pic. on p.71*

GOOSEBERRY JUICE

Grate 2-3 large Indian gooseberries and steam for 4-5 minutes. Add 4 cups water and allow to stand for 1 hour. Strain the juice and stir along with 1-2 tbsp powdered rock sugar, and a dash of powdered rock salt or black salt. Serve decorated with basil or mint leaves.

BOTTLE GOURD JUICE

Peel and chop 1 medium-sized bottle gourd and blend in a juicer along with 2 grated gooseberries (or a dash of lemon juice) and 2-3 peppercorns. Garnish with 3-4 chopped mint leaves and consume immediately to avoid discoloration.

APPLE JUICE

Peel and core 1 large apple (or ripe guava) and grind the pulp along with 1 tbsp mint leaves, 1-inch piece ginger, 1 tbsp sugar, 1 tbsp lemon juice and 1 cup water. Strain. Add 2 cups water and a dash of black salt. Serve fresh.

SUGAR SWEET COOLER

To make the Ayurvedic cooler called sharkarodaka, mix 4 cups drinking water and 1 tbsp powdered rock sugar. Add a pinch each of powdered edible camphor, pepper powder and clove powder. Stir well and serve as a cooling drink between meals.

Fruits are best consumed when ripened naturally and the best time to eat fruits is in the morning, before breakfast. Consuming a glass of fresh fruit juice after a brisk morning walk is the best way to start your day as it energizes, rehydrates and cleanses the body and mind.

SPINACH JUICE

Wash and chop 1 bunch spinach and steam for 2 minutes. Cool and blend with 3 cups water along with 2 inch piece crushed ginger in a juicer. Strain and stir in 2-3 tbsp honey, 1 tsp fresh lemon juice and salt. Consume immediately to benefit from the nutritious goodness of spinach.

RIPE MANGO JUICE

Select 2 ripe, sweet mangoes of a juicy variety of your preference. Soak in water for half an hour. This renders coolness to this fruit of hot potency. Extract pulp and blend along with powdered sugar and ½ cup boiled and cooled milk. Adjust sugar as per preference. Strain and enjoy a cup of this tasty juice. Make sure that the mangoes are sweet since Ayurvedic sutras state that sour fruits and milk do not make a healthy combination (p.63).

TANGY MANGO JUICE

Peel 1 medium-sized raw mango, chop into large slices and pressure-cook along with 1 cup water for 2 whistles or until very soft. Pass through a sieve adding 2 cups water. Grind 1 tbsp mint leaves and 1-inch piece ginger and add to the juice along with 2-3 tbsp sugar, a dash of pepper powder and powdered rock salt. Stir well and serve fresh.

KOKAM JUICE

Wash and soak 20 dry soft kokams in 4 cups water along with 2 tbsp rock sugar (or jaggery) for 1-2 hours. Now, squeeze the kokams slightly with your fingers and pass through a muslin cloth into a jug. Add ¼ tsp cumin powder and black salt to taste. Serve as a cooling drink on warm afternoons.

PLANNING MEALS

Regular meal times and sleep patterns are a sure step to good health. Ayurveda does not recommend skipping meals or maintaining rigid fasts. It also advises that one should eat when just hungry, rather than waiting until ravenous.

Early morning is the time of kapha predominance, therefore a heavy BREAKFAST is not recommended for anyone. Noon is the time of pitta predominance when digestive fire is at its highest, so a hearty LUNCH is recommended for all constitutions. An early DINNER with enough time for digestion before sleep is a good habit to cultivate in life.

Kaphas must eat a very light breakfast and a wholesome and sustaining lunch. Snacking between meals is not recommended for them. Dinner can be light and tweaked with spices.

Pittas can start their day with a light and simple breakfast. They generally feel hungry towards noon, often forgetting breakfast, so an early and hearty lunch suits them best. A light evening snack followed by a simple dinner, low on spices, is advisable for pittas as well.

Vatas must find balance by accommodating routines in their lifestyle. All their meals should be wholesome and eaten at fixed timings everyday. Snacking between meals is alright for vatas.

Below are a few examples of simple yet wholesome tridoshik menus, which means they have a good balance of dishes for a family of relatively healthy individuals.

KARE is an Ayurvedic retreat where guests come to detoxify and rejuvenate themselves. Therefore, a list of foods to be avoided has been developed for maximum benefits.

This list includes foods such as potatoes, tomatoes, cucumbers, brinjals, mushrooms, fermented batters of idli and dhokla, yeast products, preservatives, cheese, cottage cheese, pasteurized butter, buffalo milk and its products, cocoa, refined oils, fried foods, frozen foods, ice-creams, caffeine, alcohol and tobacco. However, most of these products may not be completely avoidable in daily life. So remember that one simple rule which reigns supreme - THE GOLDEN RULE OF MODERATION. As Dr. Kalmadi says, eat well-balanced meals in moderation, and you will be well on the path of sukham ayu.

BREAKFAST MENU 1
Bottle gourd juice p.105
Basic home-style chila p.85
Brahmi chutney p.96

BREAKFAST MENU 2
Spinach juice p.105
Broken wheat upma p.88
Carrot chutney p.98

LUNCH MENU 1
Home-style carrot kheer p.19
Basic home-style vegetable p.41
Basic home-style dal p.55
Rotla (with pearl millet) p.69
Basic home-style pulav p.75
Home-style chutney p.95
Spiced buttermilk p.103

LUNCH MENU 2
Khoya poli p.24
Cabbage kofta p.51
Tangy amti p.61
Mint rice p.76
Red pumpkin salad p.101
Home-style buttermilk p.102

EVENING SNACK MENU 1
Coriander wadi p.90
Spice tea p.104

EVENING SNACK MENU 2
Beaten rice upma p.89
Spinach chutney p.99
Herbal tea (see tip on p.104)

DINNER MENU 1
Clear soopa of spinach p.35
Stuffed pointed gourd p.45
Kokam kadhi p.56
Basic home style roti p.65
Goda masala pulav p.78
Coriander-mint chutney p.97
Green gram salad p.100

DINNER MENU 2
Spicy ginger-lemon soopa p.36
Tossed vegetables in milk p.46
Bottle gourd dal p.57
Rotla (with sorghum millet) p.69
Yam cutlet p.91
Spinach chutney p.99

Ayurveda tells us that food has to be eaten in proper quantity, keeping seasonal and regional availability in mind, and with all the six rasas present in every meal. This would seem like a rather tricky balancing act! How does one remember so many rules and yet eat without anxiety? Is ideal eating at all possible, one may ask.

From its vast ocean of wisdom, *Ayurveda* gives us a simple, magical answer: balance a meal in the proportion of ½ portion solid, ¼ portion liquid and ¼ portion air. This means that a meal must include solid preparations like rotis, vegetables and rice, liquid preparations like soups and dals and little sips of water as well. For air to move in the last quarter, one must stop eating just before the stomach is completely full.

FOOD GUIDE

Use the table below to choose foods that you can eat regularly (most advised), occasionally (moderately advised) and sparingly (least advised), depending on your constitution.

	VATA	PITTA	KAPHA
CEREALS, PULSES AND MILLETS			
Most advised	basmati rice, beaten rice, black gram, broken wheat, brown rice, green gram, horse gram, oats, wheat, white rice	aduki beans, basmati rice, beaten rice, broken wheat, brown rice, green gram, kidney beans, masoor gram, pearl millet, pinto beans, sanwa millet, sorghum, soya, water chestnut flour, wheat, white rice	aduki beans, barley, basmati rice, beaten rice, bengal gram, black-eyed beans, broad beans, brown rice, buck wheat, chick peas, corn, field beans, finger millet, flat beans, green gram, horse gram, masoor gram, pearl millet, pinto beans, red gram, sanwa millet, sorghum
Moderately advised	masoor gram, semolina, sorghum, vermicelli	barley, bengal gram, black-eyed beans, chick peas, dried peas, finger millet, moth beans, oats, red gram, semolina, vermicelli	broken wheat, dried peas, kidney beans, moth beans, oats, water chestnut flour, wheat, white rice
Least advised	aduki beans, barley, bengal gram, black-eyed beans, broad beans, buck wheat, chick peas, corn, dried peas, field beans, finger millet, flat beans, kidney beans, moth beans, pearl millet, pinto beans, red gram, sanwa millet, soya, water chestnut flour	black gram, broad beans, buck wheat, corn, field beans, flat beans, horse gram	black gram, semolina, soya, vermicelli
VEGETABLES AND HERBS			
Most advised	asparagus, basil, beetroot, bottle gourd, brahmi leaves, capsicum, carrot, coriander leaves, curry leaves, dill leaves, double beans, fenugreek leaves, ivy gourd, mint leaves, onion, oregano, parsley, pointed gourd, raw plantain, red pumpkin, snake gourd, sour greens (rozelle), spring onion, sunberry leaves, whitegoose foot, white pumpkin, yam	amaranth leaves, asparagus, basil, bitter gourd, bottle gourd, brahmi leaves, broccoli, brussel sprouts, cabbage, cauliflower, cluster beans, coriander leaves, curry leaves, double beans, drumstick, french beans, green peas, ivy gourd, lady's finger, lettuce, pointed gourd, raw plantain, red pumpkin, ridge gourd, snake gourd, spinach, sunberry leaves, white pumpkin	basil, bitter gourd, bottle gourd, brahmi leaves, broccoli, brussel sprouts, cabbage, capsicum, carrot, cauliflower, celery, cluster beans, coriander leaves, curry leaves, dill leaves, drumstick, fenugreek leaves, french beans, green peas, kohlrabi, lady's finger, lettuce, mint leaves, oregano, parsley, pointed gourd, spinach, sunberry leaves, whitegoose foot, yam
Moderately advised	amaranth leaves, broccoli, celery, cluster beans, colocasia, drumstick, french beans, lady's finger, lettuce, spinach, tender radish, turnips	beetroot, carrot, chayote squash, colocasia, fenugreek leaves, kohlrabi, mint leaves, onion, oregano, parsley, round gourd, spring onion, sweet potato, tender radish, whitegoose foot, yam	amaranth leaves, asparagus, beetroot, chayote squash, fresh corn, onion, raw plantain, ridge gourd, snake gourd, spring onion, tender radish, turnips, white pumpkin
Least advised	bitter gourd, brinjal, brussel sprouts, cabbage, cauliflower, chayote squash, cucumber, fresh corn, green peas, kohlrabi, mushrooms, potato, ridge gourd, round gourd, sweet potato, tomato	brinjal, capsicum, celery, cucumber, dill leaves, fresh corn, mushrooms, potato, sour greens (rozelle), tomato, turnips	brinjal, colocasia, cucumber, double beans, ivy gourd, mushrooms, potato, red pumpkin, round gourd, sour greens (rozelle), sweet potato, tomato
FRUITS AND FLOWERS			
Most advised	apricots, bananas, cherries, coconut, custard apple, figs, grapefruit, guava, Indian gooseberry, kiwi, lemon, papaya, peaches, plums, pomegranate, ripe mango, rose petals, sapota, strawberries, sweet grapes, sweet lime, sweet melon, sweet oranges, sweet pineapple, wood apple	apple, bananas, black jamun, coconut, figs, guava, Indian gooseberry, pears, pomegranate, ripe mango, rose petals, sweet grapes, sweet lime, sweet melon, sweet pineapple, water chestnut, watermelon	black jamun, cherries, custard apple, hibiscus, Indian gooseberry, lemon, papaya, pomegranate, rose petals, wood apple
Moderately advised	apple, black jamun, hibiscus, jackfruit, pears	apricots, cherries, custard apple, grapefruit, hibiscus, jackfruit, kiwi, lemon, papaya, peaches, plums, sapota, wood apple	apple, kiwi, peaches, pears, ripe mango, sweet melon, sweet pineapple
Least advised	raw mango, water chestnut, watermelon	raw mango, strawberries, sweet oranges	apricots, bananas, coconut, figs, grapefruit, guava, jackfruit, plums, sapota, strawberries, sweet grapes, sweet lime, sweet oranges, raw mango, water chestnut, watermelon

	VATA	PITTA	KAPHA
SPICES			
Most advised	asafoetida, bay leaf, black salt, caraway, cardamom, carom seeds, cinnamon, cloves, coriander seeds, cumin, dry ginger, dry mango powder, fennel seeds, fenugreek seeds, fresh ginger, garlic, mustard seeds, nigella seeds, nutmeg, peppercorns, rock salt, saffron	cloves, coriander seeds, camphor, rock salt, saffron	asafoetida, bay leaf, camphor, caraway, cardamom, carom seeds, cinnamon, cloves, coriander seeds, cumin, dry ginger, dry mango powder, fennel seeds, fenugreek seeds, garlic, green chillies, mace, mustard seeds, nigella seeds, nutmeg, peppercorns, red chillies, rock salt, saffron, turmeric
Moderately advised	camphor, green chillies, mace, poppy seeds, red chillies, turmeric	asafoetida, black salt, caraway, cardamom, carom seeds, cinnamon, cumin, dry ginger, fennel seeds, fenugreek seeds, garlic, nigella seeds, turmeric	black salt, fresh ginger, poppy seeds
Least advised	*All spices are good for vata.*	bay leaf, dry mango powder, fresh ginger, green chillies, mace, mustard seeds, nutmeg, peppercorns, poppy seeds, red chillies	*All spices are good for kapha.*
DRY FRUITS, NUTS AND SEEDS			
Most advised	almonds, cashewnuts, charole nut, dates, kokam, pistachios, pumpkin seeds, raisins, sesame seeds, tamarind, walnuts	charole nut, dates, dry figs, groundnuts, raisins, watermelon seeds	*Most dry fruits, nuts and seeds, being heavy, are not much recommended for kapha.*
Moderately advised	dry coconut, groundnuts, linseeds, sunflower seeds	almonds, cashewnuts, pistachios, sunflower seeds	charole nut, dry coconut, dry figs, kokam, raisins, tamarind
Least advised	dry figs, watermelon seeds	dry coconut, kokam, linseeds, pumpkin seeds, sesame seeds, tamarind, walnuts	almonds, cashewnuts, dates, groundnuts, linseeds, pistachios, pumpkin seeds, sesame seeds, sunflower seeds, walnuts, watermelon seeds
DAIRY, SWEETENERS, BEVERAGES			
Most advised	buttermilk, coconut milk, coconut water, cow's ghee, cow's milk, honey, jaggery, khoya, rock sugar, sugarcane, unsalted butter.	buttermilk, coconut milk, coconut water, cow's ghee, cow's milk, honey, jaggery, rock sugar, soy milk, unsalted butter	buttermilk, cow's ghee, honey, jaggery
Moderately advised	cottage cheese, soy milk, tofu, yogurt	khoya, sugarcane, tofu	coconut water, cow's milk, rock sugar, soy milk
Least advised	pasteurized butter, white sugar	cottage cheese, pasteurized butter, white sugar, yogurt	coconut milk, cottage cheese, khoya, pasteurized butter, sugarcane, tofu, unsalted butter, white sugar, yogurt
OILS			
Most advised	coconut oil, mustard oil, olive oil, sesame oil, soyabean oil	coconut oil	mustard oil
Moderately advised	groundnut oil, linseed oil, safflower oil, sunflower oil	olive oil, sesame oil, soyabean oil, sunflower oil	corn oil, sesame oil
Least advised	corn oil	corn oil, groundnut oil, linseed oil, mustard oil, safflower oil	coconut oil, groundnut oil, linseed oil, olive oil, safflower oil, soya bean oil, sunflower oil
HERBAL TEAS *refer tip on p.104*			
Most advised	aloe vera, basil, cardamom, dried ginger, fresh ginger, lemon grass, liquorice, mint leaves, rose petals, saffron, sarsaparilla	aloe vera, liquorice, rose petals, sarsaparilla	aloe vera, basil, cardamom, dried ginger, hibiscus, lemon grass, mint leaves, rose petals, saffron, sarsaparilla
Moderately advised	hibiscus	basil, cardamom, dried ginger, hibiscus, lemon grass, mint leaves, saffron	fresh ginger, liquorice
Least advised	*Teas are good for vata and keep them warm.*	fresh ginger	*All herbal teas are soothing for kapha.*

GLOSSARY of ingredients that appear in this book, based on food groups.

English, Hindi, Sanskrit

CEREALS, MILLETS, PULSES

Aduki beans, Chori
Basmati rice, Basmati, Sugandhak shali
Beaten rice, Poha, Chipita

Bengal gram, Chane ki dal, Chanaka
Black gram, Urad, Masha
Black-eyed beans, Lobiya, Rajamasha
Broken wheat, Daliya
Buck wheat, Kuttu .
Chick pea, Chole, Chanaka
Corn, Makka, Yavanala
Field, flat & broad beans, Vallar, Nishpava
Finger millet, Madua (ragi), Madhulika

Green gram, Moong, Mudga
Kidney beans, Rajma, Rajamasha
Masoor (red lentil), Masoor dal, Masura
Moth beans (aconite), Moth, Makushtha
Pearl millet, Bajra

Peas (dried), Sukhe matar, Kalaya
Red gram, Arhar dal, Adhaki
Rice, Chawal, Shali
Semolina, Sooji
Sorghum, Jowar, Joorna

Soya, Bhatvas
Vermicelli, Sevai, Sevika
Wheat, Genhu, Godhuma

rock salt

rock sugar

VEGETABLES AND HERBS

Amaranth leaves, Chauli ka saag, Tanduliya
Basil, Tulsi, Tulasi

Beetroot, Chukandar

Bitter gourd, Karela, Karvella
Bottle gourd, Lauki, Alabu
Brahmi leaves, Brahmi, Somavalli

Cabbage, Band gobhi, Kalambi
Capsicum, Shimla mirch, Maricha Phalam

Carrot, Gajar, Garjara
Cauliflower, Phool gobhi

Celery, Ajwan ka patta, Ajmoda
Chayote squash, Chow chow
Cluster beans, Gawar phali
Coriander leaves, Hara dhaniya, Dhanyaka
Corn (Fresh), Bhutta, Yavanala
Curry Leaves, Karipatte

Double Beans, Vallar, Shimbi shaak

Drumstick, Saijan ki phali, Shobhanjana phala
Fenugreek leaves, Hari methi, Methika
French beans, Faras, a variety of Shimbi
Green peas, Matar, Vartula
Ivy gourd, Tondli, Bimbi
Kohlrabi, Knol Khol
Lady's Finger (okra), Bhindi, Bhenda
Lettuce, Salad patta, Kahu
Mint leaves, Pudina, Pudina
Onion, Pyaaz, Palandu
Pointed gourd, Parval, Patola

Radish (tender), Mooli, Mulaka
Raw plantains, Kachcha kela, Apakva kadali

Red pumpkin, Kaddu, Gudayogaphala

Ridge gourd, Turai, Koshataki
Snake gourd, Chichinda, Chichinda
Spinach, Palak, Palakya

Spring onions, Pyaaz patti, Palandu shaak
Sunberry leaves, Makoy (manathakkali), Kakamachi

White pumpkin, Petha, Kushmanda
Yam, Jamikanda, Surana

FRUITS AND FLOWERS

Apple, Seb, Shimbitika
Coconut, Nariyal, Narikela
Guava, Amrood, Peruka
Hibiscus, Gudahul, Japa

Indian gooseberry, Amla, Amalaki

Lemon, Neembu, Nimbuka
Pomegranate, Anar, Dadima
Raw mango, Kachcha aam, Baala Amra
Ripe mango, Aam, Amra
Rose Petals, Gulab, Shatapatri

Water Chestnut, Singhada, Shringataka
Watermelon, Tarbooz, Kalinda

SPICES

Asafoetida, Hing, Hingu
Black salt, Kala namak, Sauvarchalam lavanam
Camphor, Kapoor, Karpura
Caraway seeds, Shah jeera, Krishna jiraka

Cardamom, Elaichi, Sukshmaila
Carom seeds, Ajwain, Yavani
Cinnamon, Dalchini, Darusita
Cloves, Laung, Lavanga
Coriander seeds, Dhaniya, Dhanyaka
Cumin seeds, Jeera, Jiraka
Dry ginger, Sonth, Sunthi
Dry mango powder, Amchur, Sushka amraphala

Fennel, Sounf, Mishreya

Fenugreek seeds, Methi, Methika
Fresh ginger, Adarak, Ardraka
Garlic, Lahasun, Rasona
Green chillies, Hari mirch, Lanka
Indian bay leaf (cassia leaf) Tej patta, Tamal patra

Mace, Javatri, Jatipatri
Mustard Seeds, Rai, Rajika
Nigella, Kalonji, Krishna jiraka
Nutmeg, Jaiphal, Jatiphala
Peppercorns, Kali mirch, Maricha

Poppy seeds, Khus khus, Khakhastila
Red chillies, Lalmirchi, Katuvira-lanka
Rock salt, Saindha namak, Saindhava lavana
Saffron, Kesar, Kunkuma
Turmeric, Haldi, Haridra

DRY FRUITS, NUTS & SEEDS

Almonds, Badam, Vatada
Cashewnut, Kaju, Kajutaka
Charole (cudpah nut), Chironji, Priyal
Dates, Khajur, Kharjura

Dry coconut, Khopra, Jeerna narikela
Groundnut, Moongphali, Mandapi

Kokam, Kokam, Vrikshamla

Pistachios, Pista, Abhishuk
Raisins, Kishmish, Draksha
Sesame, Til, Tila
Sunflower seeds, Soorajmukhi ke beej
Tamarind, Imli, Amlika

DAIRY, SWEETENERS & BEVERAGES

Buttermilk, Mattha, Takra
Coconut milk, Nariyal ka doodh, Narikela dugdham
Cow's ghee, Gaay ka ghee, Goghritam
Cow's milk, Gaay ka doodh, Godugdham
Honey, Shahad, Madhu
Jaggery, Gud, Guda

Reduced milk, Khoya, Ghana dugdham
Rock sugar, Mishri, Pushpasita
Yogurt from cow's milk, Gaay ka dahi, Godadhi

Spice Box (refer p. 92)

INDEX

In this endeavour, our deepest gratitude and appreciation to:

Our families and all our friends who understood when we buried ourselves in Ayurvedic texts for months, often ignoring their needs!

The stoic kapha, Dr. Kalmadi, who gently nudged us along, and to his ever smiling wife Ragini, for her inputs with the recipes.

The happy, wonderful team at KARE with a special mention of Dr. Roli, for those wonderful discussions and arguments, that led us to fresh understandings.

Prof. Dr. Srinivasa Rao, who to us, is beyond all doshas, for his microscopic concentration on concepts, and for teaching us to be patient with the process of learning.

Prabodh, for his vision and keen design sense, and the Envission team, for their unconditional support. Kavitha, for weaving her magic even across continents; and our dear friend, Srivatsa, for his untiring zeal.

Prasiddha that petite, no-nonsense pitta, who chugged away with unrelenting clarity as she edited our writing, and Shobha, whose witty honesty made her a very generative critic.

And those who were there at various stages of this project – Ruchika and Vrinda, for their assistance in design execution; and Nidhi, Sadhana, Sangeetha, Sneha and Tanmai for their help with all the nagging nitty-gritties.

Our destiny with Pedatha happily continues, for just as her son, Preetham, stood by us during the making of "Cooking at Home with Pedatha", this time, it was her grandson, Rohit, who first visualized us taking on this project.

We are indeed grateful and fortunate to have the blessings of Guruji Shri B.K.S. Iyengar in this project.

Jigyasa and Pratibha

*"Food when consumed without thought
can be poisonous. The same when eaten
with discrimination is the nectar of life."*
Charaka Samhita

*"We gather mere stones and call them
gems, whereas the real gems of life are
water, food and words of wisdom."*
Rig Veda

annadaata sukhi bhava